Bank-Administered, Commingled Pension Funds

Bank-Administered, Commingled Pension Funds

Performance and Characteristics, 1962-1970

Edward Malca
The City University of New York

Lexington Books
D.C. Heath and Company
Lexington, Massachusetts
Toronto   London

Library of Congress Cataloging in Publication Data

Malca, Edward.
   Bank-administered, commingled pension funds.

   Bibliography: p.
   1. Pension trusts—United States—Investments. I. Title.
HD71-6.U5M28   332.6'327   73-13566
ISBN 0-669-91181-X

Published simultaneously in Canada.

Printed in the United States of America.

International Standard Book Number: 0-669-91181-X

Library of Congress Catalog Card Number: 73-13566

Contents

List of Tables

List of Figures

Acknowledgments

During the writing of this book, there were a number of individuals who provided much helpful advice, excellent suggestions, and valuable comments. I wish to thank Mr. William Brock, Vice President of A.G. Becker and Company, who helped me to define my topic. A note of thanks is greatly deserved by Professors Peter M. Gutmann, Martin Zweig and John Zdanowicz of Baruch College. These gentlemen guided me throughout with very valuable suggestions. Further, I wish to thank Professor Hedwig Reinhardt, who first interested me in the pension fund area. I also wish to thank Professor Albert Zucker, both for his useful advice on statistical matters and for his constant encouragement.

The cooperation of all the participating banks is very deeply appreciated. Furthermore, invaluable help was obtained from Ms. Camille Lynch of the City University Computer Center on matters pertaining to computer programming.

My deepest and warmest thanks goes to my wife Jeanette, who did a superb job of editing the manuscript. Her patience, endurance and helpful advice is greatly appreciated. The support, confidence and understanding which she gave me during this period were major ingredients towards the successful completion of this study. This book is thus dedicated to my wife.

Edward Malca

1

Introduction

Private pension funds have been in existence for over a century. The enormous growth of these funds began after 1949 due to the Inland Steel decision, in which the Supreme Court of the United States refused to review a lower court decision that required employers to bargain collectively on the issue of pension plans.[1] This decision gave to the unions the right of collective bargaining on pension plans, and the stage was set for the future growth of these plans. This growth can be seen by the fact that in 1950 total assets, at book value, of private noninsured pension funds were 5 billion dollars,[2] while two decades later, in 1970, their assets totaled over 97 billion dollars.[3] Private noninsured pension funds have thus become one of the fastest growing financial institutions in the nation during the last two decades.

In February 1971, the New York Stock Exchange released a study which showed that in 1949 private noninsured pension funds held 0.5 billion dollars in common stocks—less than 1% of the market value of all New York Stock Exchange listed stocks. In 1970, on the other hand, these funds held 55 billion dollars worth of common stock, which was 8.6% of the market value of all New York Stock Exchange listed stocks.[4] In reference to the above growth, the report stated:

In an effort to improve the rate of return on their investment portfolios, pension funds have shifted an increasing proportion of their assets into common stocks. This, coupled with new money flows available each year for investment, has led pension funds to dwarf all other types [of institutional investors] in importance.[5]

In comparing total institutional holdings of New York Stock Exchange listed common stocks versus private noninsured pension fund holdings of NYSE listed common stock, we find that institutional holdings of all NYSE listed common stocks have doubled from 13% in 1949 to over 25% in 1970. In the same period, noninsured

1

private pension fund holdings increased over 900%, going from less than 1% to 8.6% of the total market value of all NYSE listed common stocks.[6]

This shift toward significant common stock investment by pension funds is a recent development. In 1964 private noninsured pension funds held the great majority of their assets in corporate or United States government bonds.[7] In an attempt to explain the above shift, West, director of research for the New York Stock Exchange, attributed it to "their [pension funds'] desire to achieve a greater return on their portfolios than was possible on fixed-income securities."[8]

In discussing the growth and importance of private pension funds, one must keep in mind that noninsured private pension funds represent the majority of these funds and that the assets of these noninsured funds are "managed largely by commercial banks."[9]

In fact, in 1970, trust departments of commercial banks administered assets having a market value of approximately 288 billion dollars.[10] Employee benefit plans accounted for over 101 billion dollars, or over one-third of total trust assets.[11] The portion of total trust assets invested in common stocks amounted to approximately 180 billion dollars. It is interesting to note that this amount exceeded the sum of the total common stocks administered by investment advisers, insurance companies, self-administered employee benefit plans, foundations, and educational endowments.[12]

As can be seen from Table 1-1, in 1960 total private pension fund assets (at book value) were 52 billion dollars. These assets were divided between noninsured plans, with 33 billion dollars, and insured plans, with 18.8 billion dollars. In other words, over 60% of total private pension fund assets were of the noninsured type, while less than 40% were of the insured type.[13] One decade later, total private pension assets (at book value) rose over 165% to 138.2 billion dollars. Noninsured plans had 97 billion dollars in assets, or over 70% of the total, while the insured plans had assets of 41 billion dollars, or under 30%. Thus, while total private pension assets increased by 166% during the last decade, the noninsured type increased by 194% while the insured type increased only 119%. It is therefore apparent that noninsured plans have increased their percentage of total pension assets (and so have the bank trust departments who are the main administrators of these funds).[14] It is estimated that by 1980 total assets of private pension plans will exceed 220 billion dollars.[15]

Table 1-1

Assets of Private Pension Funds (At Book Value-in Billions of Dollars)

	1950	1960	1961	1962	1963	1964	1965
Noninsured pension funds[a]	6.5	33.1	37.5	41.9	46.6	52.4	59.2
Insured pension reserves	5.6	18.8	20.2	21.6	23.3	25.2	27.3
Total private pension funds	12.1	52.0	57.8	63.5	69.9	77.7	86.5
Percentage of total reserves (%)							
Insured pension reserves	46.3	36.2	34.9	34.0	33.3	32.4	31.6
Noninsured pension funds[a]	53.7	63.7	65.0	66.0	66.7	67.4	68.4
	1966	1967	1968	1969	1970	1975	1980
Noninsured pension funds[a]	66.2	74.2	83.1	90.6	97.0	N.A.[b]	N.A.
Insured pension reserves	29.4	32.0	35.0	37.9	41.2	N.A.	N.A.
Total private pension funds	95.6	106.3	118.0	128.5	138.2	175.0	225.0
Percentage of total reserves (%)							
Insured pension reserves	30.8	30.1	29.7	29.5	29.7		
Noninsured pension funds[a]	69.2	69.8	70.4	70.5	70.3		

Sources: SEC Statistical Series Nos. 2516 and 2581, *Private Noninsured Pension Funds*, 1970, 1971.

President's Committee on Corporate Pension Funds and Other Private Retirement and Welfare Programs, *Public Policy and Private Pension Programs—A Report to the President on Private Employee Retirement Plans* (Washington, D.C.: G.P.O., 1964), appendix A, table 1.

Note: May not add up to totals due to rounding.

[a]Includes funds of corporations, nonprofit organizations, and multiemployer and union plans.

[b]Not available.

It is generally known that several hundred retirement plans account for a very large percentage of the total assets of all private noninsured pension plans.[16] Partly due both to higher costs and an uncertain profit outlook, smaller firms have lagged behind the larger corporations in instituting deferred compensation programs. However, in recent years the smaller companies' reserves of employee benefit plans have risen sharply as these employers have included retirement benefits as part of the wage settlement.[17] Since contributions by smaller companies to their retirement plans may be rather small, they face many problems in operating their employee retirement plans. Diversifications and liquidity may be quite difficult to obtain when annual contributions are sometimes as small as $1,000. As Bernstein stated before a Senate subcommittee:

With a small fund the investor has the problem of emphasizing either safety or yield to the detriment of the other. The diversification possible with large funds more readily promotes both safety and yield. What evidence there is indicates that small funds have a lower rate of return than more ample funds. This may be overcome by pooling funds, a service offered by some banks. But little is known about the prevalence of pools and their comparative yields.[18]

And, as Frank L. Griffin reported to the Senate Committee on Aging:

What facts do we know about private pension plans? We know that most large and medium-sized employers already have pension plans covering their employees and that there are a growing number of small employers adopting [pension] plans. . . .[19]

To help ameliorate this disadvantageous position of the smaller companies, the banks turned to a concept that was used for smaller personal trusts—that is, a pooling of assets.

Prior to 1955 this pooling could only be used for personal trusts and not for investing employee benefit plan assets. However, on June 13, 1955, Regulation F of the Federal Reserve System was changed to permit collective investments of reserves for retirement plans, provided that each participating plan was exempt from federal income tax. In 1962 the authority over these trust powers was transferred to the Comptroller of the Currency.[20]

In other words, a new method for investing the assets of smaller companies' retirement plans was started in 1955. By 1960 there were 64 banks administering commingled funds for employee benefit plans, with assets of almost 440 million dollars.[21] By 1965 the *Trusts and Estates* survey showed 122 banks administering this type of fund with assets, at book value, of almost $2.5 billion. This represented a relative increase of over 400%, while for the same five-year period, assets of private noninsured pension funds increased only by 74%.[22]

In fact, the diversity and growth of these commingled employee benefit trusts have grown so rapidly that as of September 1970, one leading New York City bank had seven different types of commingled retirement funds, ranging from bond and common stock funds to foreign securities and special situation funds. When combined, all seven of these commingled employee benefit trusts had assets of over $400 million, or almost as much as the assets of all commingled employee benefit plans in 1960.[23]

Moreover, in April 1972 First National City Bank released data on its trust department activities for the first time. It was disclosed that they administer $5.9 billion of employee benefit assets, approximately 7% of which is represented by commingled funds.[24]

Although commingled funds for employee benefit plans still represent a rather small percentage of the total bank-administered retirement plans, two distinct factors must be realized. The first is that the assets of these commingled funds are increasing at a more rapid rate than are the increases in total private retirement assets. In 1960 commingled funds represented 1.2% of total private retirement assets. In 1964 they represented 3.1%, and in 1968 it was estimated that over 6% of total private retirement assets were represented by commingled funds.[25]

The second factor that must be kept in mind is that in 1970 bank trust departments administered $288 billion, and of this amount over one-third, or roughly $101 billion, was represented by the assets of employee benefit plans.[26]

Thus, as can be seen in Table 1-2, assets of all private pension funds grew over 150%, from 52 billion dollars in 1960 to over 135 billion dollars a decade later. The noninsured funds grew approximately 190%, from 33 billion dollars to 96 billion dollars during the same period. Even though the noninsured pension funds grew enormously during the 1960s, commingled funds for employee benefit plans grew at an even faster rate. In 1960 their assets were $440 million; by 1965 they had reached $2.5 billion. It is conservatively estimated that by 1970 their assets at book value amounted to $12 billion.[27] Thus commingled funds for employee benefit plans grew over 2600% in the decade of the 1960s. This substantial growth far outpaced the growth of all noninsured private pension plans, as well as all other private pension plans. Table 1-2 provides a further breakdown of percentage increases.

Table 1-2
Percentage Changes in Pension Assets (At Book Value—Percentage)

	1960-65	1965-67	1967-70
All private pension funds	66.3	22.9	28.2
Insured pensions	45.2	17.2	26.6
Noninsured pensions	78.9	25.3	29.1
Commingled funds for employee benefit plans	468.0	156.0	87.5

Source: Data computations based upon Table 1-3.

Using Table 1-3 as a guideline, it is found that approximately $12 billion is in commingled funds. But more important is the fact that, as one leading New York City bank pension officer told this writer: "We use the same staff and they generate the same recommendations for both our regular pension fund accounts and for our commingled accounts. In general, the performance results are very similar." (Due to the bank officer's request for anonymity, no source note is provided.)

Herein lies an important reason for this entire study. It is not possible to obtain the necessary performance data for private noninsured pension funds, but since this data is generally available for bank-administered commingled funds for employee benefit plans, it is possible to use information about commingled funds to further our knowledge about bank-administered noninsured pension funds. It is assumed that this study will give us a clearer picture as to how the commingled funds performed for the 1962-70 period. However, more importantly, this study will show how the equity portions of bank-administered employee benefit plans have performed. It is unfortunate that, until Congress forces banks to make full disclosure of trust activities, this method will have to be used for studying bank-administered employee benefit plans.[28] A similar method was used by Hanczaryk when he stated his general approach:

Table 1-3
Pension Assets (At Book Value—in Billions of Dollars)

	1960	1965	1967	1970
All private pension funds	52.0	86.5	106.3	136.3
Insured pensions	18.8	27.3	32.0	40.5[a]
Noninsured pensions	33.1	59.2	74.2	95.8
Commingled funds for employee benefit plans	.44	2.5	6.4[b]	12.0[c]
Commingled funds as percentage of total private pensions	1.15%	3.1%	6%	9%

Sources: Securities and Exchange Commission Release No. 2516 *Private Noninsured Pension Funds* (Washington, D.C.: G.P.O., 1971).

Frank C. Voorheis, *MSU Business Topics*, "Investment Strategy of Pooled Funds," (Spring 1969).

[a]Estimate by Securities and Exchange Commission.

[b]Estimate by Frank C. Voorheis in MSU Business Topics, "Investment Strategy of Pooled funds," Spring 1969.

[c]Estimate based on interviews with several New York City bank vice-presidents in charge of trust operations.

More is known about trust activities of national banks than any other fiduciary, and more is known about the performance of their common trust funds than any other type of fund. We are, therefore, forced to make successive generalizations on the basis of increasingly small particulars.[29]

The writer has interviewed several leading New York City bank vice-presidents and trust officers, all of whom gave a positive response to the question, "Are similar analyses, recommendations, and decisions arrived at by the same staff for commingled funds and for pension funds?" Herein lies the greater value of this study.

Growth and Outlook for Commingled
Funds for Employee Benefit Plans

In reference to Table 1-1, it is seen that noninsured plans have been the principal method that employers have utilized for funding private pension programs. In 1950 (not shown in Table 1-1) these funds accounted for 54% of total private pension reserves, while two decades later they represented over 70% of these pension reserves.[30] In absolute terms, these noninsured pensions increased from $6.5 billion to over $95 billion during this twenty-year period.[31] Since, as previously mentioned, most noninsured pension plans are administered by bank trustees, these figures indicate quite clearly the enormous degree of authority which banks have over the investments of pension reserves.

Accompanying the increase in the assets of noninsured private pension plans has been the growth of commingled funds for employee benefit plans. Annual surveys were conducted by *Trusts and Estates* until 1965; these and later studies provide a fairly good indication of the increasing importance of commingled funds for the reserves of small-to-medium sized pension trusts. The results are summarized in Table 1-3. Shown in this table is the dramatic rise of commingled funds from under 500 million dollars in 1960 to approximately $12 billion in 1970. With small-to-medium-sized companies continually being pressured to establish pension and profit-sharing plans, the reserves of these commingled funds should continue to grow dramatically in the near future.

In reference to the necessity of setting up pensions in smaller companies, John F. Tomayko of the United Steelworkers of America stated before a Senate committee that "our [pension] problem exists chiefly among the smaller employers."[32] Or, as Professor Barbash commented before a congressional committee hearing on pensions: "In the small-employer sector . . . the union presence has made the difference between pensions and no pensions."[33]

It would seem that, with this continued pressure on smaller employers to establish retirement plans, these commingled fund reserves will increase dramatically in the years ahead.

Growth of Common Stocks as a
Component of the Portfolios
of Private Pension Funds

Significant common-stock investing by private noninsured pension funds is a relatively recent phenomenon. As late as 1957, these noninsured pension funds had a 70% to 25% mix between fixed income assets and common stocks.[34] However, in the last fifteen years, the trend has been toward significant equity investing by these funds. It can clearly be seen from Tables 1-4 and 1-5 that common stocks constitute the major portion of private noninsured pension portfolios today. This is a gain from only 35.5% of total assets in 1961 to 59% in 1971.[35] In fact, in the intervening years there was a steady increase of equity investments and a steady diminution of the importance of corporate bonds in these pension funds' portfolios. This can be seen by the increase of common stocks as a percentage of total assets, from 33% in 1960 to 44% in 1965 to 59% in 1971,[36] while for the same period corporate bond percentages decreased from 43% to 41% to 27%, respectively.

Thus, in less than fifteen years, private noninsured pension funds have changed their emphasis as to the best investment medium. They have shifted from long-term debt to equities. In fact, in 1971 these funds added, at book value, 11 billion dollars to their common-stock holdings, while their total assets increased 9.4 billion dollars. This was brought about by pension funds liquidating other portfolio investments, including corporate bonds, in order to purchase common stock.[37]

In reference to stock transactions of financial institutions,[38] it is found that, from 1960 to the present, private noninsured pension funds accounted for well over one-half of all net purchases of common stock. As can be seen in Table 1-6, these pension funds are the major institutional investors in the stock market.

Table 1-4

Assets of Private Noninsured Pension Funds (Millions of Dollars)

Book Value	1961	1962	1963	1964	1965	1966
Cash and deposits	660	710	770	890	940	900
U.S. government securities	2,720	2,920	3,050	3,190	2,990	2,750
Corporate and other bonds	16,880	18,100	19,560	21,420	23,130	25,230
Preferred stock	760	750	710	650	750	790
Common stock	13,340	15,730	18,120	20,950	25,120	29,070
Mortgages	1,560	1,880	2,220	2,780	3,380	3,910
Other assets	1,590	1,800	2,120	2,540	2,870	3,520
Total assets	37,510	41,890	46,550	52,420	59,180	66,170

Book Value	1967	1968	1969	1970	1971[a]
Cash and deposits	1,320	1,590	1,620	1,800	1,640
U.S. government securities	2,320	2,760	2,790	3,030	2,730
Corporate and other bonds	26,360	27,000	27,610	29,670	29,010
Preferred stock	980	1,330	1,760	1,740	1,770
Common stock	34,950	41,740	47,860	51,740	62,780
Mortgages	4,080	4,070	4,220	4,300	3,680
Other assets	4,230	4,580	4,720	4,730	4,800
Total assets	74,240	83,070	90,580	97,010	106,420

Source: SEC Statistical Release No. 2581, *Private Noninsured Pension Funds, 1971* (Washington, D.C.: G.P.O., April 1972).
[a]Preliminary.

Table 1-5

Assets of Private Noninsured Pension Funds (As Percentage of Total 1961, 1966, 1971)

Book Value	1961	1966	1971[a]
Cash and deposits	1.9%	1.4%	1.5%
U.S. government securities	7.2	4.2	2.6
Corporate and other bonds	45.1	38.1	27.3
Preferred stock	2.1	1.2	1.7
Common stock	35.5	44.0	59.0
Mortgages	4.3	5.9	3.5
Other assets	4.3	5.3	4.5
Total	100%	100%	100%

Source: SEC Statistical Release No. 2581, *Private Noninsured Pension Funds, 1971* (Washington, D.C.: G.P.O., April 1972).
[a]Preliminary.

Table 1-6
Purchases, Sales, and Net Acquisitions of Common Stock (Millions of Dollars)

	1960	1965	1966	1967	1968	1969	1970	1971
Private noninsured pension funds								
Purchases	2,610	5,585	6,610	10,035	12,285	15,230	13,955	21,685
Sales	670	2,560	3,165	5,655	7,815	10,270	9,370	12,800
Net purchases	1,940	3,025	3,445	4,380	4,470	4,960	4,585	8,885
% of total institutional purchases	62%	66%	71%	63%	57%	52%	54%	60%
Open-end investment companies								
Purchases	2,785	6,530	10,365	14,925	20,100	22,060	17,130	21,555
Sales	2,000	5,165	9,320	13,325	18,495	19,850	15,900	21,175
Net purchases	785	1,365	1,045	1,600	1,605	2,205	1,225	380
Life insurance companies								
Purchases	405	985	1,110	1,685	2,930	3,705	3,770	6,160
Sales	220	600	825	875	1,725	2,185	1,975	2,810
Net purchases	185	390	285	805	1,205	1,520	1,795	3,350
Property and liability insurance cos.								
Purchases	640	770	900	1,165	2,245	3,780	3,615	4,170
Sales	400	965	825	980	1,645	2,880	2,720	1,945
Net purchases	240	−190	80	185	600	900	890	2,225
Total								
Purchases	6,440	13,875	18,985	27,810	37,565	44,775	38,465	53,570
Sales	3,290	9,285	14,135	20,835	29,680	35,185	29,970	38,730
Net purchases	3,150	4,585	4,850	6,975	7,885	9,590	8,500	14,845

Source: SEC Statistical Release No. 2585, *Stock Transactions of Financial Institutions 1971*, table 1 (1972).
Note: Data rounded to nearest $5 million and may not add to totals.

This shift to common stocks as an investment vehicle has put greater emphasis upon the equity management portion of their portfolios. As was mentioned earlier, most private noninsured pension funds are administered by commercial banks. It is a noteworthy fact that, in 1971, these pension funds held over $84 billion in common stock, which is 68% of total assets.[39] These assets grew at an annual rate of 12% over the last decade, and this has placed great emphasis upon the administration of these reserves.[40] The bank trust departments are generally known to be the administrators of most of these pension assets, and they have become extremely active in equity investments. A determination of their performance is essential.

Participation in Commingled Funds
for Employee Benefit Plans

Participation in bank-administered commingled funds for employee benefit plans is open to "any pension or profit sharing plan that qualifies for tax exempt status under applicable Internal Revenue Code provisions. . . ."[41]

The second qualification most often mentioned for participation is that the bank must be named as either the trustee or cotrustee, or, at the least, as agent for the trustee.

Thirdly, the trust agreement must expressly permit the commingling of trust assets.

Today, there are many different types of commingled funds for employee benefit plans. The participants, in consultation with their trust officer, decide what portions of their fund to invest in each fund. A typical bank would have both an equity fund and a fixed income fund, as well as a special situation fund.

The Operation of Commingled
Investment Funds[42]

Upon establishment of a commingled fund for employee benefit plans, trustees of each participating plan purchase units or shares in the funds at a predetermined price, frequently $10 per unit. All deposits are then invested in a diversified portfolio, with the selection of individual securities being determined *exclusively by the bank trustees.*

Valuation of units in the fund is made as of the last business day of each selected period, usually each month or quarter. Deposits to, or withdrawals from, a pooled fund can usually be made only on these valuation dates. The value of a unit is determined in a manner similar to the one used by mutual funds. That is, the unit value is determined by obtaining the market value of the entire portfolio less any liabilities, divided by the number of units outstanding. Dividend earnings are most often reinvested as received and are reflected in the unit values at each valuation date.

Banks do not normally charge a fee for administering these pooled investment funds. The bank receives only its usual compensation for administering each individual employee benefit trust as trustee, cotrustee, or agent for the trustee.[43] This fee is generally levied either quarterly or annually and is expressed as a percentage of the market value of the assets of the participating trust. Typically, a fee schedule would be 0.5% for the first $100,000 of trust and would descend accordingly with a minimum fee of $250 annually.

Advantages of Commingled Funds as an Investment Medium[44]

There are many advantages available to small-to-medium-sized retirement plans that participate in a commingled fund. A number of these advantages are presented below:

1. *Diversification.* The collective investment of reserves of many pension and profit-sharing plans through a commingled fund offers each participating trust a greater degree of diversification in its investment portfolio. This is more than would ordinarily be possible if the reserves of each trust were invested separately. A higher degree of diversification usually results in greater stability of income and principle.
2. *Long-Term Growth.* Greater long-term growth possibilities are available to commingled funds than to small independent trusts, because sales of securities from collective funds are seldom required to meet unit withdrawals. In addition, in most funds, continuous automatic reinvestment of income further augments growth prospects of commingled funds.[45]

3. *Liquidity.* The liquidity requirements of a commingled fund are much smaller than those of a small trust because deposits to a commingled fund almost always exceed withdrawals. Consequently, a larger portion of the reserves of a commingled fund can be invested in long-term, higher-yield securities.

4. *Service Cost.* Brokerage commissions and transfer costs are generally lower for a commingled fund than for a small independent trust, since the commingled fund trades in larger blocks of securities.

5. *Yield.* Small-to-medium-sized trusts, in contrast to commingled funds, must hold a greater portion of their securities in lower-yield assets with greater liquidity. Higher-yield issues which may be available to commingled funds through private placements often cannot be obtained by small trusts.

In addition, participation in commingled funds gives the participating trust flexibility as well as an investment program especially designed to meet the needs of employee benefit trusts.[4 6]

Given these advantages of investing collectively, it is not surprising that assets of pooled funds for employee benefit plans have increased so dramatically over the last decade.

Need for Study

As related earlier, in 1970 bank trust departments managed $288 billion while in 1963 they managed an estimated $144 billion.[4 7] The growth of these bank-managed funds should give some credence to the fact that they have invested these funds wisely. Approximately one-third of the total bank trust assets represent assets of pension and profit-sharing funds. It can be seen that bank trust departments are acquiring ever-increasing responsibilities and prestige. One would think that there would be many in-depth studies in this area, and especially on employee benefit trusts, since they are of a greater public interest. However, after a thorough search of the literature, it was found that there were only a few studies related to this area. In one such study, Hanczaryk studied personal trusts, their investments and performance via an analysis of common trust funds. This study provides a basic outline of the problem, but it only deals with personal common trust funds and mentions employee benefit plans only in passing. Furthermore, Hanczaryk does not take into consideration the matter of risk when he analyzes performance.

In a related work, Friend studied mutual funds as an institutional investor. This study proved to be nothing more than an updated Wharton Study on mutual funds. Friend acknowledges his omission of the leading institutional common stock purchaser in this way: "the necessary data are not available for pension funds, the other major institutional group in the stock market."[48]

The first work that attempted to study bank-administered employee benefit plans was by Voorheis.[49] Voorheis studied forty-three bank-administered, pooled equity funds for the period 1960-64. He determined the rates of return for these funds, but he made a significant mistake in not taking *risk* into consideration in the study of performance. It is a generally accepted tenet of finance that, with increased risk, one can achieve higher returns. Thus Voorheis's neglect of risk leaves his conclusions wanting. As Friend stated in reference to mutual funds:

Not only rates of return but also the associated *risk* must be considered before one can draw more *definite* conclusions about the comparative performance of mutual funds [or pension funds] and the market as a whole.[50] (Emphasis added.)

Herein lies the greatest flaw in Voorheis's study.

Much has happened since the 1960-64 period. For one thing, these commingled funds were only in their infancy during Voorheis's study period. In fact in 1960, bank-administered, pooled funds for employee benefit plans had assets of only $440 million while in 1968 assets were estimated to be $6.5 billion. This growth alone may have caused many changes in the way these funds are managed, and thus some of Voorheis's conclusions may no longer be valid. In the late 1960s, since Voorheis's period of study, the entire investment community has emphasized performance. Thus the writer will attempt to ascertain how this affected the performance of bank-administered, commingled equity funds for employee benefit plans.

Voorheis did an excellent job of providing the ground work in this vital area of study. As he states (and as this writer concurs), the time period was too short to fully appraise bank trust departments. As Voorheis sums this up:

Five years may be too short a period to fairly appraise investment performance of bank trustees as managers of equity portfolios. Therefore, while this study of pooled equity funds has laid some groundwork for an appraisal of investment performance of bank trustees, it must by necessity be left to others, *employing a longer examination period*, to more conclusively determine if the enormous investment responsibility banks possess over reserves of private retirement plans is justified on an investment performance basis.[51] (Emphasis added.)

In a related area, the Securities and Exchange Commission studied collective funds of bank trust departments.[52] This study combined collective funds for employee benefit plans with common trust funds. Also included were both equity funds and balanced funds. Common trust funds and employee benefit plans have different investment objectives. For example, with the latter, income taxes are insignificant while with the former, income taxes are very important. Thus the results obtained from this study cannot really be indicative of either type of fund performance. Also, since both equity and balanced funds are combined, the results do not distinguish between equity- and debt-investment performance. Thus this study will be quite different from that of the SEC, since their study aggregated these different types of funds.

The following are some of the other drawbacks of the SEC study of collective funds administered by banks:

1. The study period was only for three years—1967-69. Such a short time period is inadequate to fairly appraise investment performance.[53]
2. For performance and other characteristics, this study only compiled one total average of the monthly averages for the entire three-year period. There was no further breakdown of data.
3. The study was only interested in the fifty largest banks. It thus neglected small-and-medium-sized banks which are quite active in the administering of pooled employee benefit plans.

As mentioned earlier, commingled equity funds for employee benefit plans must issue annual reports and must file them with the Comptroller of the Currency. These reports are the only semipublic records that bank trust departments issue. Thus, as one vice-president of a bank stated, "our commingled funds for employee benefit plans represent to the investing public our overall pension-fund performance."[54] In view of the above statement and in view of the writer's other interviews with bank officials, this study's major contribution will be to help sponsors of private retirement plans become better able to select the best investment medium for their funds. This will contribute to a more optimum distribution of pension fund assets.

With the increased public and congressional pressure for full bank trust department disclosures, this study will help contribute to the limited information known about this huge reservoir of trust assets. It is interesting to note that most trust department critics are "disturbed by their [trust departments'] tendency toward *overly conservative investment performance.*"[55] (Emphasis added.)

Thus this study will help to answer questions about the investment performance of bank trust departments versus other investment possibilities.

Purpose and Limitations of Study

The funds studied will only be those which were in continuous operation for the entire study period (1962-70). The list of bank-administered, commingled equity funds for employee benefit plans will be obtained from the August 1962 issue of *Trusts and Estates*. In order to determine whether these funds are still in existence, the writer will use the reference material issued by the American Bankers Association: *Collective Investment Funds: Operated under or in General Conformity with Regulation 9 of the Comptroller of the Currency*, February 1971.

This study will not deal directly with bank trust assets other than commingled equity funds for employee benefit plans, since the rest of bank trust department assets and activities are quite confidential.

The measurement of the rate of return will be similar to that used by Friend. The risk measurement to be used will be the beta coefficient of the rates of return on a quarterly basis. Such a risk measurement was recommended by Friend and Markowitz.[56,57]

In addition to measuring risk-adjusted investment performance, a further purpose of this study is to determine if risk-adjusted performance achieved by bank-administered commingled funds was related to the following factors:

1. Fund size (dollar value)
2. Portfolio activity rate
3. Bank size (total deposits)
4. Growth rate of fund assets
5. Risk (beta coefficient)
6. Degree of diversification

Through several interviews with bank vice-presidents and trust officers, the writer found a general consensus that their investment performance on commingled equity funds should exceed the market averages over a several-year period. This view is contrary to what was found by Friend for mutual funds. He states that "for the five-year period covered, the average performance by mutual funds was not appreciably better than what would have been achieved by a completely unmanaged portfolio. . . . "[58]

The hypothesis of this study is that, for the period 1962-70, bank-administered commingled equity funds for employee benefit plans performed as well as the Standard and Poor's 500 Stock Average. The above comparison is adjusted for risk factors and dividends.

The concluding hypothesis is that, adjusted for risk, New York City banks did not outperform banks outside New York City in their management of commingled equity funds for employee benefit plans. This is what would be expected based upon the efficient market model.

Conclusion and Application

This study will answer the question of how well banks administer commingled equity funds for employee benefit plans. It will also explore how well the banks fulfill their investment obligations to these plans.

As Friend states about pension funds:

Their equity investments are made with the goal of lowering the amount that employers and employees must contribute while maintaining or even increasing eventual benefits.[59]

By means of equity investments, these pension funds will hopefully lower labor expenses and will thus contribute to higher corporate profits.

This study will explore more fully the allocation of financial resources by employee benefit plans. Was the allocation at an optimum level or was it suboptimum, and thus partially misallocated?

In discussing the institutional investors, Friend asserts:

Their contribution to economic efficiency depends to a great extent on their ability to help the equity markets transfer capital into the most profitable investments in productive goods (with due allowance for differences in risk).[60]

If the results of this study show that the performance of these funds, adjusted for risk, was significantly inferior to an unmanaged portfolio with similar risk, then a strong argument can be made that the banks' enormous responsibility over pension and profit-sharing plans is unjustified. In fact, this would point to a misallocation of financial resources.[61] If these funds did significantly better than the return on an unmanaged portfolio with similar risk, then the converse will prove to be true.

The results obtained from this study will be of particular interest and importance to: pension and profit-sharing fund administrators, corporations, pension beneficiaries, and banks, as well as to other financial institutions who compete with banks for pension and for other asset reserves.

The intent of this study is to help obtain needed information in an area lacking such information. Whatever results this study provides will hopefully contribute to a more optimum distribution of investment responsibility over reserves of private retirement programs, and thus to a more optimum allocation of resources.

2

Characteristics of the Sample

Various size and growth statistics relating to both participating banks and their respective commingled equity funds are presented and analyzed in this chapter. Many of these statistics will also be utilized in subsequent chapters which contain several analyses of investment-performance characteristics.

Size Characteristics of Sample

The banks participating in this study are those that were included in the third annual survey of bank-administered commingled equity funds published by *Trusts and Estates* in August 1962. To be eligible for this study, a bank must have continually administered a commingled equity fund for the entire nine-year period of 1962 through 1970. Even though there were well over 100 banks that administered some type of commingled fund for employee benefit plans, only approximately 75 met the above-mentioned criterion. Several banks instituted their commingled equity plans after January 1, 1962, and thus did not meet the nine-year requisite of the study. Other banks maintained a "balanced" fund approach to fund investing, which included both debt and equity securities in one fund; these banks were therefore not included in this study.

In order to determine whether the approximately 75 banks were still administering these commingled equity funds, the writer checked the American Bankers' Association publication, *Collective Investment Funds: Operated under or in General Conformity with Regulation 9 of the Comptroller of the Currency, 1971*. It was determined that 72 banks were still administering these commingled equity funds.[1]

In order to obtain information concerning portfolio composition and investment performance of banks' commingled equity funds, a letter was sent to an officer of each bank. A second letter was required in cases where the initial letter was not acknowledged within forty-five days. This method was necessarily required since the Office of the Comptroller of the Currency refused to release the annual reports of bank-administered commingled funds.[2]

Trust officers of thirty-seven eligible banks agreed to participate in the study.[3] Since many of the bank officers requested that their comments and their data *not* be ascribed to their respective institutions, the names of officers and banks are accordingly withheld throughout this study.

Table 2-1 shows the number of participating banks representing the various states. This table shows that nineteen states are represented by the thirty-seven participating banks in the study. As would be expected, the participating banks are usually located in the larger cities of their respective states. For example, all five banks representing New York State have their headquarters in New York City. This is also true for Pennsylvania, where all four banks have their headquarters in Philadelphia.

Table 2-1
Distribution of Thirty-seven Participating Banks, by State

State	Number of Banks
Alabama	2
California	5
Colorado	2
Connecticut	1
Delaware	2
Hawaii	1
Illinois	1
Indiana	1
Maine	1
Maryland	1
Massachusetts	2
Minnesota	1
Missouri	2
Nebraska	2
New Mexico	1
New York	5
Ohio	2
Pennsylvania	4
Texas	1
Total Number of Participating Banks	37

Because some banks provided more information than others concerning their commingled equity fund operations, the number of funds included in each of the several analyses will vary. A breakdown of the thirty-seven banks according to type of information submitted appears below:

Data on size of participating banks	37
Data on fund size	34
Data on fund growth	33
Data on average portfolio activity rate	29
Data on investment performance	37

Asset Size of Participating Banks

Table 2-2 reveals that small banks, as well as larger banks, have actively participated in administering commingled equity funds. Banks with total assets of less than $300 million comprised 1.3% of the total deposits of all participating banks. The smaller banks administered seven, or 18.9%, of the thirty-seven funds included in this study. Over 37% of all equity funds in operation continuously since 1962 have been administered by banks with total deposits of less than $550 million. The giants of the industry, banks with total

Table 2-2

Size Classification of Participating Banks, Based Upon Total Deposits on December 31, 1970

Assets (in Millions of Dollars)	Banks		Total Deposits (in Millions of Dollars)	
	Number	Percentage	Amount	Percentage
Below $300	7	18.9	1,518	1.3
$300 and less than $550	7	18.9	3,151	2.7
$550 and less than $1,200	10	27.0	7,765	6.7
$1,200 and less than $5,000	6	16.2	15,232	13.1
$5,000 and above	7	18.9	87,466	76.0
Total	37	100%	115,132	100%

Source: Securities and Exchange Commission, *Institutional Investor Study*, 1971.

Note: Range of participating banks—total deposits December 31, 1970:
   Largest bank—$25.644 billion
   Smallest bank—$104 million
   Mean bank size—$3.2 billion

deposits above 5 billion dollars, also administered seven, or 18.9%, of the thirty-seven funds. However, these large banks represented 76% of all the deposits of participating banks. As can be seen, banks of all sizes are adequately represented in this study. Thus it is not just the very large banks that actively promote commingled equity funds—small-and-medium-sized banks are also actively involved in this area.

Asset Size of Participating Commingled Funds

Table 2-3 presents the distribution of commingled equity funds for the years 1962, 1965, and 1970. It is interesting to observe that in 1962 there were twice as many funds with assets below $2 million than there were in 1965. However, by 1970 there were no funds with assets below $2 million. In fact, at the other extreme, this tendency toward increased fund size also becomes evident. There were only two funds with assets above $45 million in both 1962 and 1965, but by 1970 there were six such commingled funds. To further explore the general pattern of asset growth experienced by these funds for the study period, Table 2-4 must be examined. Commingled funds with assets below $2 million decreased during this period as a percentage of total commingled equity assets. This reduction went from 3.5% in 1962 to 1.5% in 1965 to 0% in 1970. Funds with assets in excess of $45 million increased from 44.0% and 53.1% in 1962 and 1965 respectively to 58.2% in 1970. This demonstrates a significant growth pattern for these commingled equity funds during the study period.

The concentration statistics presented in Table 2-5 reveal the

Table 2-3
Distribution of Commingled Equity Funds by Total Assets within Each Class Size (at Market Value)

Assets (in Millions of Dollars)	1962	1965	1970
Below $2	12	6	0
$2 and less than $10	19	13	11
$10 and less than $25	0	13	12
$25 and less than $45	1	0	5
$45 and above	2	2	6
Total	34	34	34

Table 2-4

Distribution of Commingled Equity Funds by Total Fund Assets and Percentage in Each Size Class (at Market Value)

Assets (in Millions of Dollars)	Total Fund Assets (at Market Value) (in Millions of Dollars)			Percentage of Total Assets		
	1962	1965	1970	1962	1965	1970
Below $2	8,290	7,685	0	3.5	1.5	0
$2 and less than $10	90,014	75,912	54,924	37.9	1.5	5.4
$10 and less than $25	0	159,080	233,065	0	30.7	23.1
$25 and less than $45	34,681	0	134,576	14.6	0	13.3
$45 and above	104,441	275,284	588,286	44.0	53.1	58.2
Total	237,426	517,961	1,010,851	100.0	100.0	100.0

Table 2-5

Percentage of Total Assets of Thirty-four-Commingled Funds Held by the Largest Two Funds, Largest Six Funds, and Largest Ten Funds (in Millions of Dollars)

	1962		1965		1970	
	Total Assets	Percentage	Total Assets	Percentage	Total Assets	Percentage
Largest 2	104	43.9	221	42.7	305	30.2
Largest 6	164	69.2	321	62.0	588	58.2
Largest 10	188	79.3	376	72.6	722	71.4
Total Assets (34 Funds)	237		518		1,011	

'degree of disparity existing among the thirty-four participating commingled funds. The two largest commingled funds accounted for over 40% of all fund assets for 1962 and 1965. However, in 1970 their percentage was drastically reduced to 30.2%.[4] The largest six funds accounted for over 60% of total fund assets for both 1962 and 1965. In 1970 this percentage fell to 58.2%. The largest ten funds consistently controlled more than 70% of total fund assets for each of the years 1962, 1965, and 1970. Although this does indicate that concentration was rather high, some deconcentration did occur, especially during the years 1965-70, as can be seen in Table 2-5. The data in Table 2-5 shows a rather high degree of concentration over the study period, with a tendency toward deconcentration during the last five-year period.

The relationship between size of commingled equity funds and size of administering banks is presented in Table 2-6. Size ranking of banks is based upon total deposits as of December 31, 1970. Asset ranking of funds is based upon total fund assets as of the end of 1970.[5] As would be expected, there tends to be a direct relationship between the size of the commingled equity fund and the size of the administering bank. Over 80% of all funds with assets less than $10 million were administered by banks in the smallest size categories, while over 80% of all funds in excess of $45 million were adminis-tered by banks in the two largest size groupings. Testing to find out whether this relationship is statistically significant, it is found that the simple correlation coefficient (r) between bank size and fund size is 0.63 with a t value of 4.56, which is significant at the 99% level.

Asset Growth of Participating Commingled Funds

Table 2-7 depicts the phenomenal asset growth of commingled equity funds classified by bank asset size for the eight-year period of this study. It is interesting to note that the greatest percentage growth was among the funds with total assets of below $5 million.

The data in Table 2-8 reveals a considerable degree of disparity

Table 2-6

Relationship between Size of Pooled Equity Funds and Size of Administering Banks as of December 31, 1970

Total Deposits of Administering Bank (in Millions of Dollars)	A	B	C	D	Total Number of Banks
Below $300	6	1			7
$300 and less than $550	3	3	1		7
$550 and less than $1,200	2	4	2	1	9
$1,200 and less than $5,000		3		1	4
$5,000 and above		1	1	4	6
Total Number of Funds	11	12	4	6	33

Note:

A = Funds with total assets of less than $10 million.
B = Funds with total assets of $10 million and less than $25 million.
C = Funds with total assets of $25 million and less than $45 million.
D = Funds with total assets of $45 million and above.

Table 2-7

Thirty-three-Commingled Fund Percentage Growth: December 31, 1962-September 30, 1970, by Fund Asset Size

As of the end of 1970 Assets (in Millions of Dollars)	Percentage Growth				
	Below 125%	125-200%	200-400%	400-800%	Above 800%
Below $5	1		2	3	1
$5 and less than $10		1	3		
$10 and less than $15	1		5	5	1
$25 and less than $45			2	2	
$45 and above		2	1	1	2
Total	2	3	13	11	4
As of the end of 1962					
Below $5	1	1	8	9	4
$5 and less than $10			4	2	
$10 and less than $25	1				
$25 and less than $45		1			
$45 and above		1	1		
Total	2	3	13	11	4

Table 2-8

Distribution of Thirty-three-Commingled Equity Funds by Average Annual Compound Rates of Growth in Total Assets over the Eight-Year Period (End of 1962-70)

Average Annual Compound Rate of Growth of Total Assets (%)	Number of Funds	Percentage of Total Funds
Less than 15%	5	15.2
15% and less than 20%	6	18.2
20% and less than 30%	14	42.4
30% and less than 40%	5	15.2
40% and over	3	9.1
Total	33	

between rates of asset growth experienced by individual funds over the eight-year period. It shows a frequency distribution of asset growth rates determined on an average annual compound rate basis. Five funds, representing 15.2% of the sample, had asset growth rates of less than 15%. Three funds, or 9.1% of the sample, had asset growth rates of over 40%. The arithmetic mean of the average annual compound growth rate is 24.2%. This encompasses a minimum growth rate of 6.3% and a maximum rate of 44.9%.

Table 2-9 illustrates the average annual compound fund asset growth rate classified by fund size. This table reveals significant differences between average asset growth rates as demonstrated by the five asset size classifications of funds. Funds with total assets of $30 million or more grew annually at about 13%, which was substantially lower than the compound rate of growth of all funds combined. The mean rate of growth for all funds was 24%. The smallest size classification, which is less than $2 million in fund assets, experienced the largest average annual growth rate—almost 28%. These findings on growth rates tend to explain the slight decline in concentration during the period 1962 to 1970, as noted in Table 2-5. Since the smaller funds were growing at a more rapid rate than the larger ones, there tended to be a decrease in the larger funds' relative share of all commingled fund assets. The smaller funds tended to increase their relative share of the total fund assets throughout the study period.

Data revealed in Table 2-9 tends to indicate a weak inverse relationship between fund size and fund asset growth rates. This can be explained by the fact that a 1 million dollar fund can increase 50% more easily than can a 50 million dollar fund.

Table 2-9
Average Annual Compound Rate of Growth of Total Assets of Commingled Equity Funds, by Size Class (End of 1962-70)

Fund Size, Total Assets (in Millions of Dollars)[a]	Number of Funds	Average Annual Compound Growth Rate[b] (%)
Less than $2	11	27.9
$2 and less than $5	12	25.6
$5 and less than $15	7	20.4
$15 and less than $30	0	—
$30 and above	3	13.1
Total	33	24.2

[a]Size classification based upon total assets at end of year, 1962.
[b]Based upon unweighted arithmetic mean of funds within each size classification.

3

Procedure, Methodology, and Historical Review

In order to measure performance of commingled equity funds for employee benefit plans, it is first necessary to discuss and explain the methodology to be used in this study. The methods used here are similar to those of several recent studies.[1]

Development of Portfolio Evaluation Theory

The methodology employed in this study would not be possible without the pioneering work in portfolio management by Harry M. Markowitz.[2] Markowitz developed the concept of "portfolio efficiency." This involves portfolios which satisfy the dual criteria of (1) highest expected return for a given level of risk and (2) lowest level of risk for a given level of expected return. This leads to a family of portfolios called "efficient sets" or "efficient frontier." That is, if risk (variability of expected return) is measured and if covariance among securities is accounted for, the efficient set of portfolios is comprised of those combinations of securities in which, for a given amount of risk, there is no other portfolio that provides higher expected return. Conversely, for a given expected return there is no portfolio that carries less risk.

Figure 3-1 presents the efficient set, in which no other portfolio at risk level σ_j provides higher expected return than R_j. Portfolio J is efficient, as are all the portfolios on the line of the efficient set.

Markowitz developed sophisticated mathematical techniques in order to obtain the efficient set. The application of his theory was all but impossible because of the great number of assessments involved. Markowitz suggested a means of substantially reducing the input requirement by making the additional assumption that security returns were jointly normal and related only through a common normally distributed market factor.[3]

Sharpe simplified Markowitz's model into a usable form by utilizing the above assumption.[4] He developed a single index or

27

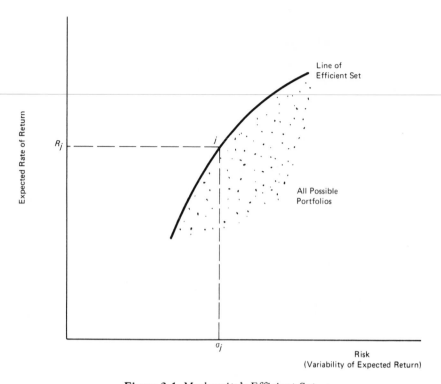

Figure 3-1. Markowitz's Efficient Set

market model in which he assumed that, through diversification, residual risk could be reduced greatly, and thus is assumed to be zero.

Sharpe's Single Index Model

$$\text{Performance measure} = \frac{\overline{R} - R^*}{S} \qquad (3.1)$$

Where:

$\overline{R}$ = average rate of return of fund for period
S = standard deviation from average return
R^* = is assumed to be the "riskless" rate

The above formula demonstrates that the higher the value of the performance measure, the better was the performance of the portfolio during the investment horizon. It should be noted that Sharpe uses the standard deviation as a measure of portfolio risk. This can be separated into two components. The first is systematic risk, which measures the riskiness inherent in the market, and the second component is residual risk, which is unique to the particular portfolio involved.

Using Formula (3.1), Sharpe studied the performance of thirty-four mutual funds for a ten-year period. His equation finds the reward provided to the investor for bearing risk. Thus Sharpe brought Markowitz from the realm of theory to actual practical application.

The capital asset pricing model was almost simultaneously developed by Sharpe, Lintner and Treynor.[5],[6],[7] This model explains that, in equilibrium, the expected return on a portfolio or security is a linear function of the covariance of its returns with that of the market portfolio. Thus letting

$\tilde{R}_j$ = return on the jth portfolio or security
R^* = the rate of return on a riskless asset
$\tilde{R}_m$ = the return on the market portfolio

Then:

$$E(\tilde{R}_j) = R^* + \frac{E(\tilde{R}_m) - R^*}{\sigma^2(\tilde{R}_m)} \; \text{cov}(\tilde{R}_j \tilde{R}_m) \qquad (3.2)$$

Therefore, the expected return on a risky security or on a portfolio of risky securities is equal to the return on a riskless asset plus an additional return for bearing risk. This is true when $[(E(\tilde{R}_m) - R^*)] / \sigma^2(\tilde{R}_m)$ is the market price per unit of risk, and cov $(\tilde{R}_j \tilde{R}_m)$ is the measure of risk associated with the jth portfolio or security.

By defining:

$$B_j = \frac{\text{cov}(\tilde{R}_j \tilde{R}_m)}{\sigma^2(\tilde{R}_m)}$$

Equation (3.2) may be rewritten as

$$E(\tilde{R}_j) = R^* + [E(\tilde{R}_m) - R^*]B_j \qquad (3.3)$$

B_j is the systematic risk of the jth portfolio and represents the extent to which the return on portfolio j is dependent upon the returns of the securities in the market. The balance of the risk associated with the jth portfolio is unique to that portfolio. It is not priced by the market, since the combination of securities in efficient portfolios eliminates this residual element of risk. Thus the risk which is unique to the security in a well-diversified portfolio is eliminated.[8]

Treynor was the first to apply a model using systematic risk.[9] In his model, he assumes a well-diversified portfolio, and hence residual risk is not considered.

Treynor's Model

$$\text{Performance measure} = \frac{R_j - R^*}{b_j} \qquad (3.4)$$

Where:

R_j = return on jth portfolio
R^* = return on riskless asset
b_j = systematic or market risk of portfolio slope of the regression line

Treynor's volatility model is exactly like Sharpe's single index model, (Equation 3.1) except that Treynor used only systematic risk while Sharpe used total risk. These are equivalent measures of performance for fully-diversified portfolios.[10]

Most recently, Jensen used the capital-asset pricing model to evaluate portfolio managers' performance.[11] He studied the performance of 115 mutual funds over a twenty-year period to determine whether their level of systematic risk in the portfolio was consistent with their rate of return.

Jensen used a method very similar to Equation (3.3), but he worked with excess yields $(\tilde{R}_j - R^*)$ and $(\tilde{R}_m - R^*)$. Jensen developed the following regression model:

$$R_j - R^* = \alpha + B_j(\tilde{R}_m - R^*) + e_j \qquad (3.5)$$

In this model, α and B_j are the intercept and slope terms, respectively, of a least square line, and e_j is a random term with zero mean. The reasoning behind Jensen's model suggests that, if the portfolio manager is a superior predictor of security prices, then the intercept term will turn out to be positive. Moreover, if the least square line is based upon past performance, α becomes a good method for ranking and comparing ex post performance.[12] Both Jensen and Treymor only considered systematic risk, since residual risk is assumed to be zero in a well-diversified portfolio.

Jensen tested to see whether the beta coefficient (B_j) is stationary over time, and he found it to be so. Treynor, Levy, and Blume tested the stationarity of beta over time and found their results to be similar to Jensen's.[13]

Thus Jensen developed a composite measure which demonstrated that, the higher the α is for a given portfolio, the better is the risk-adjusted investment performance. A method very similar to the one developed by Jensen will be used in this study; this method will be presented in detail further in the chapter.

Smith tested the Jensen, Treynor, and Sharpe composite measures to determine whether they give similar rankings. Using a rank correlation test, he concluded that there was agreement on ranking between all three measures.[14]

Thus the development of portfolio evaluation and performance has been greatly advanced by Markowitz, Sharpe, Treynor, and Lintner.[15] This summary of the development of the theory of portfolio evaluation and performance provides a background for the remainder of this chapter, which will discuss the methodology and procedures to be followed throughout this study.

Methodology

The statistical procedures to be followed will be similar to those employed in several recent studies of open-end investment companies.[16]

The writer will measure the rate of return on a quarterly basis for each fund during the nine-year period 1962-70.

Investment Performance Equation
with Dividend Reinvestment

$$R_t = \frac{MK_t - MK_{t-1}}{MK_{t-1}} \qquad (3.6)$$

Where:

R_t = rate of return for period t
MK_t = market value of net assets per fund unit at the end of period t
MK_{t-1} = market value of net assets per fund unit at the beginning of period t

This assumes continual reinvestment of dividends, which is the common practice for most commingled equity funds.

Formula (3.6) is inappropriate for measuring investment return for some commingled equity funds, since dividend income is distributed to unit holders rather than being reinvested in additional issues. To compensate for the dividend income per unit, and to take into consideration the compound effect, the following formula is employed:

Investment Performance Equation
with Dividends Distributed

$$R_t = \frac{MK_t - MK_{t-1} + \frac{1}{2}DI_t \frac{(MK_t + DI_t) + \frac{1}{2}DI_t}{MK_{t-1}}}{MK_{t-1}}$$

Where:

DI_t = dividend income distributed during period t

This measures investment return when dividend income of a commingled equity fund is distributed to unit holders.[17] The above formula is based upon two assumptions. First, it is assumed that dividend income per unit is received at a constant rate throughout the period, and that it is immediately reinvested. Employing this assumption, on the average one-half of the dividend income per unit is reinvested for the entire period of income-producing securities. Second, it is assumed that the rate of return earned on the portion of the dividend income which is reinvested for the entire period is equal to the rate of return earned on the fund units themselves. Commenting upon the above formula, Voorheis states, "the formula on balance provides a measure of investment performance very comparable to that obtained for income retention funds."[18]

The above formula for measuring investment performance of dividend payout funds will also be utilized for measuring the investment performance of the Standard and Poor's 500 Stock Average.

In order to better understand the true nature of investment performance, this study will employ the procedure for measuring risk-adjusted performance that is similar to the one recommended and used by the Securities and Exchange Commission in its *Institutional Investor Study*.[19] In this procedure, the performance measurement takes into consideration not only the rate of return, but also the level or risk taken and the "risk-free" rate of return.[20,21]

In order to obtain the return for the amount of risk taken, the writer will convert both fund returns and market return (S & P 500 Stock Average) into "risk premiums." This will be done for each quarter by subtracting the return on "risk-free" treasury bill rates from the fund returns and from the market returns.[22]

Risk Premiums

$$R_{sm} = R_m - R_b \qquad (3.8)$$

$$R_{st} = R_t - R_b \qquad (3.9)$$

Where:

R_{sm} = risk premium for market index
R_{st} = risk premium for fund
R_m = rate of return for market index for period
R_t = rate of return for fund for period
R_b = three-month treasury bill rate

The risk premiums will provide the rate of return for the amount of risk taken.

The volatility estimate of each fund is the risk measure known as the beta coefficient. In order to obtain this, one must plot each fund's risk premiums along the vertical axis of a chart, while the market's risk premium must be plotted along the horizontal axis. By method of least squares, the writer will fit a regression line to the scatter chart—the resultant slope is the basic risk measure known as the beta coefficient. See Equation (3.10). Figure 3-2 presents graphically this risk measurement.

$$R_{st} = a + B_i (R_{sm}) \qquad (3.10)$$

The beta coefficient "is a measure of systematic or nondiversifiable risk, i.e., the dispersion in return that cannot be reduced through market diversification."[2 3] It "measures the way in which the return on a portfolio tends to follow the overall market."[2 4] The beta coefficient is a volatility measure of the sensitivity of the portfolio to movements in the general market.

The next step is to compute a volatility adjusted performance rating—the performance measure technically known as alpha (α). This is necessary in order to adjust the rate of return with the risk involved.

*Equation for Volatility Adjusted
Comparison Standard Portfolio*

$$R_s = R_b + B (R_m - R_b) \qquad (3.11)$$

Where:

R_s = return on the volatility-adjusted comparison standard
R_m = return on the market portfolio
R_b = return on three-month treasury bill portfolio
B = beta coefficient—volatility coefficient (or the fraction of the standard portfolio invested in the market)

To obtain the volatility-adjusted performance measure (alpha), a comparison standard portfolio is developed for each fund which has

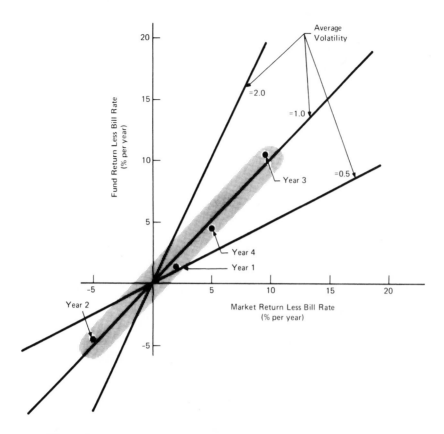

Figure 3-2. Measurement of Fund Volatility. Source: SEC, *Institutional Investor Study*, vol. 2 (1971), p. 407.

the same volatility (beta coefficient) as the fund itself.[25] The return on the performance standard is given by the sum of the return on treasury bills during the quarter plus the fund's volatility coefficient (beta) multiplied by the difference between the return on the market portfolio and return on the treasury bills during the quarter (see Equation 3.11).[26] This gives the rate of return on a hypothetical portfolio which has the same volatility as the fund.

In order to obtain a true risk-adjusted performance measure, the excess return (performance measure = alpha) must be found for each fund. This performance measure is the difference between the average return on the fund less the average return on the comparison portfolio standard (see Equation 3.12).

$$\bar{R}_t - \bar{R}_s = \alpha \qquad (3.12)$$

Where:

$\bar{R}_t$ = mean quarterly rate of return of each fund for the study period

$\bar{R}_s$ = mean quarterly rate of return of the comparison standard portfolio for the study period

α = risk-adjusted performance measure

If this performance measure (alpha) is positive, the fund has outperformed an unmanaged portfolio of similar average volatility. Conversely, if alpha is negative, the fund has performed less well than the comparison unmanaged portfolio. Obviously, the higher the positive alpha, the better the fund performance (see Figure 3-3). In a recent study on mutual funds, it was found that only 27% of those funds studied had positive alphas, or excess returns. The average alpha for mutual funds in this study was minus 2% per annum.[2][7]

This method of evaluating commingled equity fund performance will determine the performance of the funds for the amount of risk taken.

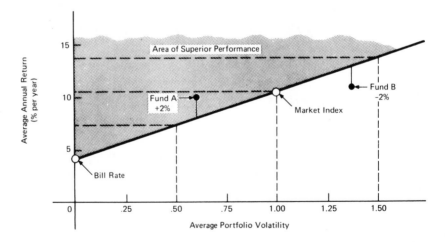

Figure 3-3. Evaluation of Fund Performance. Source: SEC, *Institutional Investor Study*, vol. 2 (1971), p. 406.

In order to provide better insight into bank-administered commingled equity funds for employee benefit plans, a comparison will be made between the relationship of the performance and the characteristics of these plans. Through use of regression analysis, the writer will determine whether the following variables are associated with risk-adjusted performance (alpha):

1. Fund size—total assets at the end of the period
2. Bank size—total deposits at the end of the period
3. Portfolio activity rate

$$\text{Activity rate} = \frac{P_t + S_t \quad / \ 2}{MK_t + MK_{t-1} \quad /2} \qquad (3.13)$$

Where:

P_t = total equity purchases in period t
S_t = total equity sales in period t

This portfolio activity rate "reflects all trading, including trading resulting from net accumulation or liquidations of stock."[2 8]

4. Volatility measure—beta coefficient
5. Risk-adjusted performance measure (alpha) in prior period
6. Average annual compound rate of growth of fund assets
7. Comparison of performance of New York City banks with banks located outside of New York City

In so testing the above characteristics of commingled equity funds, this study will ascertain whether any of the above variables significantly affect fund performance.

Review of Related Studies

Since 1963, assets under the management of trust departments grew from $144 billion to nearly $290 billion.[2 9] Of the total bank trust assets, approximately one-third represent assets of employee benefit funds. Therefore, bank trust departments are acquiring ever-increasing prestige and responsibilities. One would think there would be many studies in this rapidly growing area. However, after a thorough search of the literature, it was found that there were surprisingly few.

Hanczaryk examined personal trusts for the period 1963-68, and he studied their investments and performance via an analysis of common trust funds.[30] He found that, for the 1963-68 period, all equity common trust funds, "on the average total performance . . . [percentage change in unit share value plus yields], were superior to the Standard and Poor's Stock Price Index plus dividend yields."[31] This study only provides a basic outline of the problem (see Chapter 1, the subsection, "Need for Study").

As mentioned earlier, Friend studied mutual funds and other institutional investors.[32] His method of determining mutual-fund performance is quite similar to the one employed in this study.[33] Friend found that, in all risk classes, mutual funds performed more poorly than did a comparison standard portfolio with similar risk.[34] However, this study proved to be an updated Wharton Study on mutual funds using new performance techniques.

Jensen studied 115 mutual funds for the period 1945-64. He concluded that, on the average, mutual funds were not able to predict security prices well enough to outperform a buy-the-market-and-hold policy.[35] Also, he found "that there is very little evidence that any individual fund was able to do significantly better than that which we expected from mere random chance."[36]

It is obvious, therefore, that most recent studies using systematic risk-adjusted performance measurements concluded that, on average, these funds did no better than a risk-adjusted market portfolio. In fact, there is some evidence that these funds did slightly poorer than would be indicated by the risk they took.[37]

Voorheis studied forty-three bank-administered pooled equity funds for the period 1960-64 (see Chapter 1, subsection, "Need for Study.").[38] His study found that, on average, bank-administered, pooled equity funds did outperform the Dow Jones Average but did not outperform the Standard and Poor's 500 Stock Average for the study period. Since the late 1960s, the entire investment community has emphasized performance, and thus this may have altered the performance of bank-administered, commingled equity funds for employee benefit plans.

Another recent study in this area was done by the Security and Exchange Commission.[39] As part of their study of institutional investors, the SEC examined the investment performance of bank trust departments' collective funds. Using monthly data, forty-eight collective funds were analyzed during the period 1967-69.[40] The study concluded that, on the average, these collective funds performed slightly poorer than did a market portfolio with similar risk.[41,42] However, it was also found that portfolios for funds with higher volatility (risk) had a clear tendency to have higher measures of performance.[43] It is noteworthy that there was a statistically significant negative correlation between portfolio turnover and performance. Furthermore, there was a significant negative correlation between portfolio diversification and performance.[44]

This study combined pooled funds for employee benefit plans with common trust funds; also included were both equity and balanced funds. Common trust funds and employee benefit plan funds have different investment objectives. For example, with the latter, income taxes are insignificant while with the former, income taxes are quite important. Thus the results obtained from this study cannot really be indicative of either type of fund performance. Also, since equity and balanced funds are combined, the results do not fully distinguish between equity- and debt-investment performance.

The SEC only studied these funds for the three-year period 1967-69, and such a short time period is inadequate to fairly appraise investment performance.[45] This study was solely interested in the fifty largest banks. It neglected the small-and-medium-sized banks which are quite active in this field, and in so doing, has reduced the significance of its findings.

In the following chapter, the results of findings on the performance and the characteristics of bank-administered, commingled equity funds will be presented.

4 Investment Performance

The level of investment performance attained by commingled equity funds for employee benefit plans ultimately determines not only the benefits received by employees, but also the cost of the plan to the employer. In fact, it has been estimated that a 1% increase in investment return will generally increase benefits about 25% or decrease costs approximately 20%.[1] Given the significant impact that investment performance has on both the employers and employees, it is of paramount importance that the sponsors of employee benefit plans be cognizant of their plans' relative investment performance. In so doing, they will be able to contribute to a more efficient allocation of financial resources.

In order to measure true investment performance, one must not only consider rates of return, but must also consider risk. Thus, throughout this chapter, when performance is measured, it will be adjusted for risk.

The basic risk measure employed—technically known as the beta coefficient—"is a measure of systematic or non-diversifiable risk, i.e., the dispersion in return which cannot be reduced through market diversification."[2] This method of risk (volatility) adjustment has been employed in several recent studies of institutional investors and is fully described in Chapter 3.[3]

As stated earlier, the period of study under examination is from January 1, 1962, through September 30, 1970. This 105-month period is sufficiently lengthy to give a valid appraisal of fund performance. Within this period, one finds that the stock market had several market cycles, as approximated by the Standard and Poor's 500 Stock Average. A low was reached in mid-1962, and a peak occurred at the end of the year 1965. A new low for the market was registered at the end of 1966, while the market peaked by the end of 1968, and subsequently, the market fell sharply by midyear 1970. Thus this period will be a good indicator of investment performance because of its varied market cycles.

Investment Results

The investment performance of commingled equity funds is based on quarterly data for the period January 1, 1962, through September 30, 1970. The performance measure includes all dividends and capital appreciation for the quarter, and the risk measure (volatility) is the beta coefficient that measures systematic or market risk.[4]

As can be seen from Table 4-1, the mean beta coefficient is 0.96, which indicates that the average commingled fund had slightly less risk than the market. The maximum and minimum beta are 1.17 and 0.70, respectively. Small beta coefficients correspond to small risks. A beta of one has similar risk to a portfolio of Standard and Poor's 500 Stock Average. (See appendix, Table A-1 for the volatility measure—beta—of the 1962-70, 1962-65 and 1966-70 periods for all thirty-seven funds.)

The performance measure calculated for each fund is its quarterly rate of return minus the rate that would have been earned on an equivalent-risk combination. This risk combination is composed of a portfolio of risk-free securities (90-day treasury bills) plus the market portfolio (represented by the Standard and Poor's composite average including dividends).[5]

Table 4-1
Distribution of Volatility Measure (Beta) by Size Class[a]

Assets (in Millions of Dollars)	No. of Funds	(a)	(b)	(c)	Average Beta[b]
Less than $5	6	2	4	–	.84
$5 and less than $15	8	–	6	2	.95
$15 and less than $25	9	3	3	3	.95
$25 and less than $45	4	–	1	3	1.04
$45 and above	6	–	1	5	1.07
Totals	33	5	15	13	.96

Note:
(a) .70 ≤ beta < .85
(b) .85 ≤ beta < 1.0
(c) 1.0 ≤ beta < 1.2
Mean beta coefficient = .96
Maximum beta coefficient = 1.17
Minimum beta coefficient = .70

[a]Size classification based upon total assets as of end of year 1970.
[b]Based upon unweighted arithmetic means of funds within each size classification.

Tables 4-2 and 4-3 present a summary of the performance measure technically known as alpha (α). Specifically, Table 4-3 stratifies the performance by risk class. As can be seen, these commingled funds had a negative alpha of -0.39% quarterly, or approximately -1.6% per annum. This indicates that, on average, these funds earned about -1.6% less per year than they should have earned considering their level of systematic risk (beta). It is also clear that the distribution is skewed to·the low side with thirty funds having $\alpha_i < 0$ and only seven funds having $\alpha_i > 0$. (See appendix Table A-2 for performance of all thirty-seven funds for the 1962-70 period.)

Table 4-2
Distribution of Performance Measure (Alpha)[a] Period—January 1, 1962 through September 30, 1970

Performance Measure Alpha	Number of Funds	Mean Alpha
.01 ⩽ alpha < .02	1	+.0156
.00 ⩽ alpha < .01	6	+.0031
−.01 < alpha ⩽ .00	28	−.0053
−.02 < alpha ⩽ −.01	2	−.0143
Total	37	−.0039

Note:
Mean alpha = −.0039
Maximum alpha = +.0156
Minimum alpha = −.0152
[a]On a quarterly basis.

Table 4-3
Distribution of Performance Measure—Alpha[a] by Risk Class (Beta Coefficient)

Performance Measure Alpha	Risk Class—Beta Coefficient (a)	(b)	(c)
.01 ⩽ alpha < .02	−	−	1
.00 ⩽ alpha < .01	−	1	5
−.01 < alpha ⩽ .00	4	17	7
−.02 < alpha ⩽ −.01	1	1	−
Totals	5	19	13

Note:
(a) .70 ⩽ beta < .85
(b) .85 ⩽ beta < 1.0
(c) 1.0 ⩽ beta < 1.2
[a]On a quarterly basis.

This model implies that, with a random selection buy-and-hold policy, one should expect on average to do no worse than $\alpha = 0$. Therefore, it appears from the preponderance of negative alphas that the funds are not able to forecast future security prices well enough to recover their management fees and commission expenses.[6]

In several recent studies on mutual funds, Jensen and Levy used similar methodology and found that the mean alphas were -1.1% and -2.0%, respectively, per annum.[7] Furthermore, the SEC *Institutional Investor Study* found an alpha of -0.12% per annum for collective-investment funds of forty-eight banks.[8]

Table 4-4 presents the performance measure alpha (α) for the period January 1, 1962, through December 31, 1965, as well as for January 1, 1966, through September 30, 1970.[9] It shows that, for the 1962-65 period, the average alpha was -0.55% quarterly or approximately -2.2% per annum. For the latter period, the average alpha was -0.32% quarterly or approximately -1.3% per annum. This reaffirms the fact that, on average, commingled equity funds earned less than they should have, considering their level of risk. (See appendix Table A-2 for the performance results of the 1962-65 and 1966-70 periods.)

As can be seen from Table 4-4, the extremes in performance measure were most pronounced during the 1966-70 period, a time in which investment performance was greatly emphasized. This period had the lowest mean alpha while also having the greatest number of funds with $\alpha > 0$.

Table 4-4
Distribution of the Performance Measure, Alpha for the Two Periods—January 1, 1962 to December 31, 1965 and January 1, 1966 to September 30, 1970

Performance Measure Alpha	Number of Funds		Mean Alpha	
	1962-65	1966-70	1962-65	1966-70
$.01 \leqslant$ alpha $< .03$	–	3	–	+.0179
$.00 \leqslant$ alpha $< .01$	3	8	+.0014	+.0023
$-.01 <$ alpha $\leqslant .00$	29	19	−.0052	−.0045
$-.03 <$ alpha $\leqslant -.01$	5	7	−.0113	−.0152
Total	37	37	−.0055	−.0032

Note:

	1962-65	1966-70
Maximum alpha	+.0019	+.0224
Minimum alpha	−.0133	−.0265

As can be seen from these results, the bank-administered, commingled equity funds have performed more poorly than would be expected, given their level of risk. This is consistent with several recent studies on the performance of institutional investors.[10] These findings tend to confirm a possible misallocation of financial resources.

**Characteristics of Commingled Equity
Funds for Employee Benefit Plans**

*Description of Data Base and Definition
of Variables*

The quarterly data which was compiled describes six aspects of bank-administered equity funds for the period January 1, 1962, through September 30, 1970. This data was obtained from the annual reports of the individual banks administering these funds. There are twenty-nine funds in which complete data is available to compile the necessary variables. These variables were also computed for the subperiods January 1, 1962, through December 1965 and January 1, 1966, through September 30, 1970. The following is a detailed description of each of the variables used in this study:

1. *Performance.* A volatility-adjusted performance figure was computed for each fund on a quarterly basis.[11] Each fund has three performance figures, one for the entire period 1962-70, plus one for each subperiod.
2. *Fund Activity Rate.* This was obtained by computing the average of the annual purchases and sales divided by the average holdings for the year.
3. *Total Net Asset Value of Fund.* This is the total market value of equity assets as presented in the annual reports. The end-of-period-year net asset value was used for this study.
4. *Bank Size.* The total deposits of each administering bank were obtained from the SEC *Institutional Investor Study*. For the purposes of this study, end-of-period-year bank size is used.
5. *Volatility of Fund (beta).* As discussed in Chapter 3, this is a measure of the average volatility of each fund relative to the return in the Standard and Poor's 500 Stock Price Average. The

volatility for each fund was computed from data on quarterly fund returns and from returns on the Standard and Poor's 500 Stock Average for the 1962-70 period. Quarterly returns for the Standard and Poor's Average were adjusted for the average quarterly dividend yield.

6. *Growth Rate*. This is the average annual compound increase in total fund net assets for the study period. Beginning and end-of-period fund size were used to obtain this growth rate.

7. *Diversification Measure (R^2)*. The degree of diversification in each fund's portfolio is measured by examining the extent to which the variance in fund return is explained by movements in the market index. If a portfolio's R^2 is low, the portfolio varies substantially from the market.

Description of Regression Model

The question under examination is whether a significant portion of differences in performance can be explained by systematic differences in one or more of the six independent variables described above. Previous studies on performance found that fund size, turnover rate, and size of administering bank generally had little or no effect upon performance.[1,2] A noteworthy departure from these findings is presented in several recent studies which suggest an inverse relationship between performance and portfolio turnover, degree of diversification, and sales charges.[13,14,15] This section focuses upon the relationships between fund performance and the independent variables.[16]

The method used in preparing the data for regression analysis is as follows: For the twenty-nine funds with complete data, the mean of each variable was computed for each period. Thus the performance measures become the average quarterly returns during the study periods.[17]

The data collected were gathered mainly from these funds' annual reports—however, some data were compiled by the administering bank.

Discussion of Regression Results

Tables 4-5, 4-6, and 4-7 summarize the performance regression results. Three regressions were run—one for the entire study period

Table 4-5

Regression Performance Statistics, 1962-70: Dependent Variable, Equity Fund Performance (Alpha)

Independent Variable	Coefficient	t Value
Volatility Measure (beta)	.0439	5.485
Diversification (R^2)	−.0260	−1.825
Fund Size	−.00000	−.977
Bank Size	−.00000	−.117
Fund Growth Rate (%)	.00000	.020
Portfolio Activity Rate	.0020	.7163

Note:
R^2 = .61
Constant = −.02325

Table 4-6

Regression Performance Statistics, 1966-70: Dependent Variable, Equity Fund Performance (Alpha)

Independent Variable	Coefficient	t Value
Volatility Measure (beta)	.0388	5.73
Diversification (R^2)	−.0037	−.25
Fund Size	−.0000	−.204
Bank Size	.0000	.39
Fund Growth Rate (%)	.0000	.46
Portfolio Activity Rate	.0000	.02

Note:
R^2 = .66
Constant = −.0339

Table 4-7

Regression Performance Statistics, 1962-65: Dependent Variable, Equity Fund Performance (Alpha)

Independent Variable	Coefficient	t Value
Volatility Measure (beta)	.0035	.42
Diversification (R^2)	.0076	.62
Fund Size	.0000	.69
Bank Size	−.0000	−2.51
Fund Growth Rate (%)	.0000	.25
Portfolio Activity Rate	.0014	.19

Note:
R^2 = .30
Constant = −.00117

and one for each of the two subperiods. The period from January 1, 1962, to September 30, 1970, will be referred to as period one. The period from January 1, 1962, to December 31, 1965, will be considered period two, and from January 1, 1966, to September 30, 1970, will be known as period three. The following is a discussion of the significant results.

In the recent SEC *Institutional Investor Study*, there was found to be a clear positive relationship between higher volatility (beta) and higher investment performance for both registered investment companies and bank-managed collective funds.[18] In Table 4-8, one can see a tendency in period one for higher volatility (beta) to be associated with better performance (alpha). For periods one and three, a strong positive relationship exists between volatility and performance. This relationship has less than 1 chance in 100 of having arisen by chance. However, for period two no statistically significant relationship was found between performance and volatility. The SEC noted a similar finding for the period 1960-64 for registered investment companies.[19] This result can perhaps be explained by Blume and Friend, who found a negative relationship between mutual fund volatility (beta) and rate of return for the period 1960-64.[20] Ofer found a similar result for individual securities in the years 1961, 1963, and 1965.[21] Blume and Friend provide

Table 4-8
Distribution of the Performance Measure (Alpha) by Risk Class (Beta)[a]

Risk Class	Performance Measure				
(Beta Coefficient)	(a)	(b)	(c)	(d)	Mean Alpha
.7 and less than .85	–	–	4	1	−.0096
.85 and less than 1.0	–	1	17	1	−.0053
1.0 and less than 1.2	1	5	7	–	+.0004
Total	1	6	28	2	−.0039

Note:
(a) $.01 \leqslant alpha < .02$
(b) $.00 \leqslant alpha < .01$
(c) $-.01 < alpha \leqslant .00$
(d) $-.02 < alpha \leqslant -.01$
Mean alpha = −.0039
Maximum alpha = +.0156
Minimum alpha = −.0152
[a]Based on quarterly data for the period January 1, 1962, through September 30, 1970.

a possible explanation that for the 1960-64 period investors wrongly predicted rates of return.[22]

The finding of a strong positive relationship between volatility and performance for periods one and three is consistent with recent studies.[23] A possible explanation for this relationship might be that those commingled funds with higher risk (beta) were better able to predict the market, and thus used market timing to increase their investment performance. The fact that this strong relationship was not found for period two may be interpreted to mean that this superior ability to predict the market is not consistent over time.

In several previous studies it was found that there was no consistent relationship between performance and fund size.[24] The findings of this study show that for all three periods there was no statistically significant relationship, at the 95% level, between performance and fund size.[25]

The issue of fund size has received much attention in recent years. As Friend states:

Some loss in investment flexibility is associated with very large size. The need to purchase portfolio securities in very large blocks may take substantial amounts of time, so that investment opportunities are lost, and even in the short run may drive up the price of the securities involved beyond the level at which they were initially attractive. If the portfolio holdings are sufficiently large, the decision to sell may again take substantial time to implement, since the alternative could be a major break in the market for the issue.[26]

In essence, the key disadvantage to large fund size is that it seems to reduce investment flexibility. These theoretical considerations are not substantiated by the findings of this study.

In the recent SEC *Institutional Investor Study*, it was found that there was no significant relationship between performance of collective funds and the size of the administering banks.[27] The findings of this study generally confirm the SEC results. For both periods one and three, no significant relationship was found between performance and size of administering bank (see Table 4-9). However, for period two there was a negative relationship between performance and size of administering bank. This was found to be significant at the 95% level but not at the 99% level.

It would seem that the larger banks would have larger and better-staffed research departments, and thus would obtain better investment performance in contrast to smaller banks. This superior

Table 4-9

Distribution of Performance Measure by Commingled Fund Size,[a] 1962-70

Fund Size Total Assets (in Millions of Dollars)	Number of Funds	(a)	(b)	(c)	(d)
Less than $5	6	–	1	4	1
$5 and less than $15	9	–	2	7	–
$15 and less than $25	9	1	–	8	–
$25 and less than $45	4	–	3	1	–
$45 and above	5	–	–	5	–
Total	33	1	6	25	1

Note:

(a) $.01 \leqslant$ alpha $< .02$

(b) $.00 \leqslant$ alpha $< .01$

(c) $-.01 <$ alpha $\leqslant .00$

(d) $-.02 <$ alpha $\leqslant -.01$

[a]Based on total assets at end of the year 1970, at market value.

position should tend to help these larger banks achieve better investment performance in the administering of commingled funds. However, in testing this proposition, it is found that there is no consistent relationship between investment performance and bank size. In fact, for period two there is a slight inverse relationship between performance and bank size.[28] This may be explained by the fact that these smaller banks had a more conservative investment policy and that for most of this period low-risk portfolios outperformed high-risk portfolios.[29] A more likely explanation is that the overall relationship between performance and bank size is not consistent over time, since the findings for period two are not highly statistically significant, and since the findings for the other two periods show no statistically significant relationship. Basically, the size of the bank administering these funds is not a significant variable to help explain investment performance. (See Table 4-10 for a distribution of performance by bank size for the 1962-70 period.)

As can be seen from Tables 4-11 and 4-12, these commingled fund portfolios generally had a high degree of diversification (R^2). In other words, a high degree of the fund volatility can be explained by the market. The mean R^2 of 0.87 indicates that 87% of the variation in these portfolios can be explained by the market movements. The recent SEC study found that there was a statistically significant

Table 4-10
Distribution of Performance Measure (Alpha) by Bank Size[a]

Bank Size (in Millions of Dollars)	Number of Funds	Performance Measure			
		(a)	(b)	(c)	(d)
Below $300	6	–	1	4	1
$300 and less than $550	7	–	1	6	–
$550 and less than $1,200	9	–	2	7	–
$1,200 and less than $5,000	6	–	1	5	–
$5,000 and above	8	–	1	6	1
Total	36	–	6	28	2

Note:
(a) $.01 \leqslant alpha < .02$
(b) $.00 \leqslant alpha < .01$
(c) $-.01 < alpha \leqslant .00$
(d) $-.02 < alpha \leqslant -.01$
[a]Total deposits as of December 31, 1970.

Table 4-11
Distribution of Diversification Measure (R^2), by Performance Measure, Alpha[a]
(1962-70)

R^2	Performance Measure			
	(a)	(b)	(c)	(d)
.6 and less than .7	–	–	–	1
.7 and less than .8	1	–	2	–
.8 and less than .9	–	5	12	1
.9 and above	–	1	14	–
Total	1	6	28	2

Note:
(a) $.01 \leqslant alpha < .02$
(b) $.00 \leqslant alpha < .01$
(c) $-.01 < alpha \leqslant .00$
(d) $-.02 < alpha \leqslant -.01$
[a]For the period January 1, 1962, through September 30, 1970.

inverse relationship between diversification (R^2) and performance. The SEC offers the possible explanation that superior performance requires management efforts to be concentrated on a relatively small number of issues. It states that "the relatively diversified funds may have tracked unmanaged market portfolios more closely."[30]

Table 4-12
Distribution of Diversification Measure (R^2)[a] 1962-70

(R^2)	Number of Funds	Mean Value
.6 and less than .7	1	.681
.7 and less than .8	3	.753
.8 and less than .9	18	.871
.9 and above	15	.915
Total	37	.874

Note:

Mean R^2 = .874

Maximum R^2 = .935

Minimum R^2 = .681

[a]R^2 indicates the extent to which the variance in fund return is explained by movements in the market index.

For the 1962-70 period, the results of this study are consistent with the SEC findings of an inverse relationship between diversification and performance. This weak relationship is statistically supported at the 90% level but *not* at the 95% level of significance. For periods two and three, no statistically significant relationship is found between performance and diversification. The level of diversification also does not seem to be an important variable in explaining the differences in performance over time.

As discussed in Chapter 2, the compound annual growth rate of commingled funds varied from over 44% to less than 7% (see Table 4-13). This disparity could possibly be related to investment performance on the theory that better performance will attract a larger influx of funds. The findings reveal no statistically significant relationship between growth in fund size and investment performance for the entire period and for each subperiod. This tends to support the fact that investment performance is not the significant criterion for choosing a bank trust department. The more likely explanation for these findings is that these administrators of employee benefit plans do not have access to the relative performance of other bank trust departments and thus cannot make an intelligent investment decision. This study will help to fill this gap and will provide needed information in this area.

The *portfolio activity rate* is "defined as the average of purchases and sales of equities divided by average market value of stock holdings."[31] Just as other financial institutions increased their

Table 4-13

Distribution of Performance Measure (Alpha) by Compound Annual Rate of Growth of Total Assets of Fund[a]

Compound Annual Growth Rate of Fund Assets (%)	Number of Funds	Performance Measure				Mean Growth Rate
		(a)	(b)	(c)	(d)	
Below 15	5	–	1	4	–	10.3%
15 and less than 20	6	1	1	4	–	17.8%
20 and less than 30	13	–	4	9	–	24.9%
30 and less than 40	5	–	–	4	1	31.6%
40 and above	3	–	–	3	–	44.5%
Total	32	1	6	24	1	24.0%

Note:

(a) $.01 \leqslant alpha < .02$

(b) $.00 \leqslant alpha < .01$

(c) $-.01 < alpha \leqslant .00$

(d) $-.02 < alpha \leqslant .01$

Maximum growth rate = 44.9%

Minimum growth rate = 6.3%

[a]At market value for the 1962-70 period.

activity rates during the 1960s, so have these commingled funds significantly increased their activity rates. The mean portfolio activity rate is 0.38 with a maximum of 1.76 and a minimum of 0.10 for the 1963-70 period (see Table 4-14). It is interesting to note that this mean activity rate for commingled funds is substantially higher than the average activity rate for all financial institutions except mutual funds.[32] Table 4-15 presents the average activity rates of selected financial institutions for the period 1964-71.

Since higher activity rates lead to higher transaction costs, this would tend to lower performance unless the funds could take advantage of investment opportunities through more successful trading.

In several recent studies of institutional investors, it was found that there is a negative relationship between turnover rates and performance.[33] That is, higher turnover rates are associated with poorer performance. In contrast, however, two other studies found that there was little, if any, relationship between turnover rates and performance.[34] Thus it can be seen that there are conflicting results in this area.

This study concludes that there is no statistically significant

Table 4-14

Distribution of Average Annual Activity Rate,[a] Classified by the Performance Measure (Alpha), Eight-Year Period, 1963-70

Performance Measure (Alpha)	Average Annual Activity Rate			
	Below .2	.2 to .4	.4 to .6	.6 and Above
.02 and less than .01	–	–	1	–
.01 and less than .00	2	2	1	1
−.005 and less than .00	1	7	1	–
−.01 and less than −.005	1	6	1	2
−.02 and less than −.01	–	1	–	–
Total	4	16	4	3

Note:

Mean activity rate = .38

Maximum activity rate = 1.76

Minimum activity rate = .10

[a]Activity Rate = $\dfrac{\text{Purchases} + \text{Sales}}{2}$

$$\frac{\text{Market value}_t + \text{Market value}_{t-1}}{2}$$

relationship between portfolio activity rate and performance for the period 1963-70 and for the two subperiods (see Tables 4-5, 4-6, and 4-7). Since there is no inverse relationship, what may be indicated here is that the funds with higher turnover rates must be profiting sufficiently from this increased activity to cover the increased transaction costs.

The Wharton study concluded that, for the five-year period 1953-58, the average performance by mutual funds was not appreciably better than what would have been achieved by a completely unmanaged portfolio with the same distribution between stocks and other assets. Ever since these results were revealed, the investment community has tried to disprove these conclusions.[35] A further unwelcome finding to the investment community is the random walk theory, which postulates:

that at any given moment in time, the next period price change is random with respect to the state of knowledge at this moment . . . and that the current price fully reflects the present state of knowledge in the sense that it is equal to the [discounted] mean value of the distribution of the next period price as given by the present state of knowledge.[36]

Table 4-15
Common Stock Activity Rates for Selected Financial Institutions

Annual	Private Noninsured Pension Funds	Open-End Investment Companies	Life Insurance Companies	Property and Liability Insurance Companies	Total Selected Institutions
1964	10.6	18.2	11.8	7.8	12.9
1965	11.4	21.8	13.8	8.2	14.7
1966	12.6	34.0	16.0	8.6	19.8
1967	17.2	40.7	18.2	9.7	24.7
1968	18.7	48.4	26.8	16.0	29.4
1969	21.3	51.0	29.4	26.7	32.4
1970	20.5	45.6	27.8	28.1	29.8
1971	22.4	48.2	30.9	22.7	30.9
Mean 1964-71	16.8	38.5	21.8	16.0	24.3

Source: Securities and Exchange Commission, *Stock Transactions of Financial Institutions, 1971* (April 1972), table 3.

Partly in response to the above findings, two recent studies of institutional investment performance found that there was virtually no relationship between the performance for a given fund in one period and performance in the following period.[37] In fact, one of these studies found a slight association between good performance in one period and poor performance during the following period.[38] Funds that performed well in one period showed no consistent ability to do so in the subsequent period.

This study finds that the relationship between performance in one period and the subsequent period was such that there was a slight negative correlation. The correlation coefficient (r) is -0.132 and t value is -2.283, which is statistically significant at the 95% level. This finding tends to support the SEC conclusion that there is a slight negative association for registered investment companies between performance in one period and that in the subsequent period. The findings of this study, in conjunction with the results found by Friend and the SEC, give support to the random walk theory, which states that there is no consistent relationship between performance in one period and performance in the following period. Thus it seems that a fund can only achieve consistently higher returns than the market when it invests in high-risk securities.

The final item to be investigated examines whether the New York City banks outperformed banks outside New York City. There are several reasons for this inquiry. First, it is generally known that New York City bank trust departments manage over one-half of all noninsured private pension funds.[39] It would be assumed that, to command this position, banks would demonstrate above-average performance. Secondly, because of their size and their immediacy to Wall Street, one would expect these banks to have expert research investment and trust staffs. This expertise should tend to produce above-average performance for these New York City banks.

Included in this study are five New York City banks and thirty-two banks which are outside New York City. The null hypothesis (Ho) is that there is no difference between the performance of banks either in New York City or those outside of it. A two-tailed t test is employed to examine this hypothesis. Testing for the differences in means, it is found that there is no evidence of a statistical difference between the performance of commingled funds managed by New York City banks and those managed by banks outside New York City.[40]   Thus the null hypothesis is not rejected.

This conclusion tends to indicate that New York City banks administer the majority of pension trust assets for reasons other than performance. One of these reasons may be the banks' proximity to a significant number of corporate headquarters. Another possible explanation is that the banks have "old-line" ties with corporate entities which are not necessarily based upon performance. Still another reason may be that these corporate-fund sponsors do not have full knowledge of the risk-adjusted investment performance of the banks involved. In any event, there is no statistically supported difference between the performance of New York City bank-administered plans and the performance of those outside New York City. This tends to support the fact that there may be a misallocation of the financial resources involved.

5 Summary and Conclusions

This concluding chapter incorporates and summarizes the results found throughout this analysis of bank-administered, commingled equity funds for employee benefit plans. Such a procedure is helpful in attaining an overview of this study.

In Chapter 1, the writer introduced and discussed the growth of private pension funds as an institutional investor. In so doing, it was shown that noninsured pension funds are growing more rapidly and have significantly more assets than do their insured counterparts. In fact in 1970, over 70% of all private pension reserves were held by noninsured plans.[1] Furthermore, in the last decade these noninsured funds emphasized common stock investing to the point where they are now the major institutional purchaser of equities each year.

It is generally known that commercial-bank trust departments administer the bulk of noninsured pension reserves. Thus, with noninsured pension funds placing such an emphasis upon equities, there has been increased emphasis upon the equity investment performance of bank trust departments. Unfortunately, little is known about this performance, since the data is quite confidential in this area.

In an attempt to evaluate equity performance of bank trust departments, this study analyzed the performance of their commingled equity funds for employee benefit plans. These commingled funds have grown from approximately 1% in 1960 to 9% of total private pension assets in 1970.[2]

Interviews were conducted with bank vice-presidents in charge of trust operations, and it was found that they expect very similar returns for their commingled equity funds as they expect for the equity portions of their regular pensions. As one trust officer stated, "This is our public exposure."

The empirical examination included thirty-seven commingled equity funds of the possible seventy-two that have been in operation continuously since January 1, 1962. None of these commingled funds began operation prior to 1956.

Almost all funds doubled in asset size during the study period.[3] The average compound growth rate of fund assets was 24%, with a range of 6.3% to 44.9%. During the years of the study, it was found that there was a slight deconcentration of assets among the largest funds. This can be explained by the finding which showed that the smaller funds grew at a more rapid rate than the larger funds. This inverse relationship proved to be statistically significant.

On the inception date for the study period, January 1, 1962, the asset size ranged from below 250 thousand dollars to above 50 million dollars, with the majority of the funds below $10 million. By 1970 there was no fund with assets below $2 million, and most funds were in the category below $25 million in total assets. It was found that there is a direct relationship between the asset size of commingled equity funds and the size of the banks which administer these funds.[4]

Investment Performance

The method used to determine the investment performance is similar to that employed by the Securities and Exchange Commission's *Institutional Investor Study*.[5] Using quarterly data, the average quarterly rate of return is found. The beta coefficient is used to determine the systematic risk assumed by each fund. The writer proceeded to calculate the performance measure (risk-adjusted alpha) by obtaining both the quarterly rates of return and the risk measure (beta coefficient). This performance measure "represents the average incremental rate of return on the portfolio per unit of time which is due solely to the manager's ability to forecast future security prices."[6]

$$r_t - r_b = \alpha_i + \beta_i (r_m - r_b) \qquad (5.1)[7]$$

Where:

r_m = return on the market portfolio (S & P 500 Stock Average)
r_b = three-month treasury bill rate
β_i = beta coefficient: systematic risk
r_t = return on fund for period t
α_i = risk adjusted performance measure (alpha)

If the results are positive after calculating alpha, then the fund performed better than did an unmanaged portfolio with similar risk. The reverse is also true—a negative alpha indicates that the fund performed more poorly than did an unmanaged portfolio with similar risk.

It was found that, on average, the commingled equity funds had a beta coefficient of 0.96, which is slightly less than the risk for the market in general. The range was from 0.70 to 1.16.

With the use of Equation (5.1) as shown above, it was found that the mean alpha was -0.0039 quarterly or approximately -0.0156 annually for the study period. This demonstrates that these commingled funds had an approximately 1.6% lower return than would be expected from the risk taken. This conclusion seems to be consistent with several recent studies of institutional investors which found the mean risk-adjusted alpha to be negative.[8] It was also found that, for this period, there were seven funds with positive alphas and thirty with negative alphas. The range of these alphas was from approximately -6.1% to $+6.3\%$ per annum.

It was found that, for the period of January 1, 1962, through December 31, 1965, the mean performance measure was -0.0055 quarterly with only three funds having positive alphas and thirty-four having negative ones. For the second half of the period, January 1, 1966, through September 30, 1970, the number of positive alphas increased to eleven. However, the mean performance measure still remained negative (-0.0032 quarterly). This tends to substantiate the fact that throughout the study period, these funds did not perform as well as an unmanaged portfolio with similar risk.

It was determined that there was no relationship between performance in one year and performance the following year. This indicates that there was no fund which consistently outperformed the market, adjusted for risk.

Upon examination of the entire study period, it was determined that there was no direct statistically significant relationship between fund size and performance. Also, no statistically significant relationship was found between average annual compound growth rate of fund assets and performance. One would think that better performance would lead to a larger inflow of funds, but this was not supported by the conclusions arrived at in this study.

No direct relationship was found between the size of the banks administering commingled reserves and the performance of these reserves. If there were any relationship, it would be a slight inverse association between performance and bank size. However, this relationship was found not to be consistent over time. This finding raises the question of why the larger banks administer such a disproportionate amount of pension reserves. The answer seems not to be based upon performance.

It was demonstrated that funds with higher volatility tended to have higher measures of performance. However, this was not consistent in all periods. This is a similar result to that found by the SEC.[9]

During the study period, there was no relationship found between performance and portfolio activity rates, nor between performance and diversification measure (R^2). It is noteworthy that over 87% of the average volatility of these funds was explained by movements in the market.

Since New York City banks command a leading position in the administration of private pensions, the writer tested their mean performance to determine whether they outperformed banks outside New York City. No statistically significant difference was found between the performance of New York City banks and the performance of those banks outside New York City. This finding tends to question whether these New York banks should hold this commanding position over pension reserves.

Conclusions

Before one can fully understand the conclusions of this study, one must realize its limitations. The study dealt only with bank-administered, commingled equity funds for employee benefit plans. This was necessitated by the fact that other pension data was not available. Furthermore, the study was limited to equity performance and did not take bond performance into consideration.

It was stated in Chapter 1 that an investigation into the risk-adjusted performance of commingled equity funds would help foster a better allocation of financial resources. The results of this study show that the performance of these commingled funds was inferior to the performance of unmanaged portfolios with similar risk. This tends to demonstrate that the bank trust departments do not have the ability to forecast future security prices. Moreover, their ability to forecast security prices is further questioned since there is no relationship between performance in one year and in the following year.

The conclusion for the study period is that the performance of commingled equity funds has been inferior to what would have been achieved by an unmanaged portfolio of similar risk. Thus the null hypothesis, which states that these funds performed as well as the market adjusted for risk, must be rejected. This concludes that the allocation of these funds to bank trust departments is at a sub-optimum level. Thus they are partially misallocated, since an unmanaged portfolio of similar risk would have performed better.

One pertinent finding was that higher-risk portfolios outperformed lower-risk portfolios after adjusting for differences in risk. This was not fully consistent in all periods. Further research should be initiated in this area to determine whether or not this relationship is consistent over a longer time period.

A further purpose of this study was to find whether the administration of these pension reserves by New York City banks is justified by performance. Performance was found not to be the justification—perhaps it is due to other factors such as location and "old-line" ties.

What is still needed in this field is an all-inclusive study of private pension-fund performance. Also needed is a thorough analysis of bank trust departments, which are the largest administrators of equity assets. This will not be possible until Congress passes laws that require trust departments to make public the annual reports on their operations. Today, this field is cloaked with secrecy, but because of the enormous wealth and the public nature of these pension funds, this information *must* be made available. This is necessary to determine whether the allocation of these pension reserves is at an optimum level.

Appendixes

Table A-1
Distribution of Beta Coefficient (Volatility Measure)

1962-70	1962-65	1966-70
.902	.937	.893
.857	.851	.844
1.122	1.189	1.157
.982	1.016	.967
1.011	1.030	1.019
.995	1.079	.937
.942	1.011	.890
.853	.964	.811
1.090	1.112	1.134
.931	1.004	.896
.922	.927	.923
.990	1.097	.942
.815	.704	.868
1.098	1.097	1.119
.877	1.046	.775
.726	.572	.788
.876	.687	.988
.978	.900	1.032
1.048	.976	1.090
1.167	1.013	.1324
.797	.903	.746
.823	.972	.736
1.113	1.148	1.122
.965	.957	.979
.703	.811	.615
1.108	1.105	1.118
1.096	1.078	1.121
1.133	1.221	1.097
1.000	1.060	.996
1.010	1.164	.935
1.003	1.131	.955
.861	.937	.823
.993	.985	.992
.948	.943	.966
.858	1.029	.719
.927	.923	.901
.950	1.004	.924

Table A-2
Distribution of the Performance Measure (Alpha)

1962-70	1962-65	1966-70
+.0002	−.0017	+.0016
−.0042	+.0007	−.0077
+.0156	+.0019	+.0102
−.0033	−.0038	−.0034
−.0035	−.0071	−.0001
−.0045	−.0022	−.0007
−.0070	−.0041	−.0117
−.0055	−.0091	−.0040
+.0099	−.0009	+.0212
−.0079	−.0088	−.0084
−.0068	−.0074	−.0062
−.0005	−.0024	−.0007
−.0073	−.0061	−.0064
−.0032	−.0133	+0013
−.0070	−.0051	−.0126
−.0152	−.0111	−.0165
−.0068	−.0088	−.0008
−.0049	−.0070	−.0008
−.0042	−.0048	−.0020
+.0038	−.0102	+.0224
−.0096	−.0111	−.0103
−.0097	−.0107	−.0143
+.0016	−.0040	+.0035
−.0073	−.0092	−.0051
−.0061	−.0003	−.0145
−.0051	−.0065	−.0034
−.0011	−.0039	+.0023
+.0017	−.0008	+.0045
−.0037	−.0092	+.0010
−.00731	−.0089	−.0088
+.00109	−.0030	+.0028
−.0067	−.0072	−.0077
−.0059	−.0048	−.0069
−.0021	−.0050	+.0013
−.0133	−.0045	−.0265
−.0036	+.0016	−.0091
−.0034	−.0040	−.0037

Table A-3
Distribution of the Average Number of Issues in the Commingled Fund Portfolio

	Study Periods[a]	
	1962-65	1966-70
Mean number of issues	60	50
Maximum number of issues	104	80
Minimum number of issues	28	26
Number of funds in this sample	30	30

[a]Study periods: a. January 1, 1962 through December 31, 1965.
                 b. January 1, 1966 through September 30, 1970.

Table A-4
Distribution of Average Turnover Rates[a] by Performance Measure (Alpha) for the Period 1963-70

Performance Measure (Alpha)	Turnover Rates[b]			
	Below .1	.1 to .3	.3 to .5	.5 and above
.02 and less than .01	—	—	1	—
.01 and less than .00	1	3	1	1
−.005 and less than .00	2	5	2	—
−.01 and less than −.005	1	4	3	2
−.02 and less than −.01	—	1	—	—
	4	13	7	3

Note:

Mean turnover rate = .30

Maximum turnover rate = 1.67

Minimum turnover rate = .04

[a]Turnover rate = $\dfrac{\text{lesser of purchases or sales}}{\text{market value at the beginning of the year}}$

                   market value at the end of the year

                   divided by two

[b]Average for the eight-year period, 1963-70.

Notes

Notes

Chapter 1
Introduction

1. *Inland Steel Company v. National Labor Relations Board*, 170 F 7d (7th Cir. 1948) Cert. Denied, 336 U.S. 960 (1949).

2. Victor Andrews, Irwin Friend, and Hyman Minsky, *Private Capital Market* (Englewood Cliffs, N.J.: Prentice-Hall, 1964), p. 389.

3. Securities and Exchange Commission, Statistical Release No. 2581, *Private Noninsured Pension Funds* (1971).

4. The New York Stock Exchange Research Report, "Institutional Holdings of NYSE–Listed Stocks," (1970).

5. Ibid.

6. Ibid.

7. SEC Statistical Release No. 2581.

8. *New York Times*, March 1, 1971, p. 44.

9. Edwin Hanczaryk, Comptroller Staff Reports, *Bank Trusts: Investments and Performance*, Office of the Comptroller, Washington, D.C., pp. 8-9.

10. Trust Assets Total $288 Billion in Latest FDIC Survey," *Trusts and Estates*, January 1972, p. 27.

11. Ibid.

12. Securities and Exchange Commission, *Institutional Investor Report*, vol. 2 (Washington, D.C.: G.P.O., 1971).

13. SEC Release No. 2516.

14. Hanczaryk, *Bank Trusts.*

15. President's Committee on Corporate Pension Funds and Other Private Retirement and Welfare Plans, *Public Policy and Private Pension Programs, A Report to the President on Private Employee Plans*, table 1, appendix A, (Washington, D.C.: G.P.O., 1965).

16. Frank Voorheis, "Investment Strategy of Pooled Funds," *MSU Business Topics* (Spring 1969), p. 25.

17. Ibid., p. 27.

18. U.S., Congress, Senate, Subcommittee on Employment and Retirement Incomes of the Special Committee on Aging, *Extending Private Pension Coverage*, Hearing, Statement of Merton C. Bernstein, pt. I, 85th Cong., 1st sess., 1965.

19. U.S., Congress, Senate, Special Committee on the Aging,

Economics of Aging: Towards a Full Share in Abundance, pt. 10B, 91st Cong., 2d sess., February 18, 1970, p. 1649.

20. U.S., Treasury Department, *101st Annual Report,* Comptroller of the Currency (Washington, D.C.: G.P.O., 1963), p. 13.

21. Annual Survey of Bank Administered Pooled Funds for Employee Benefit Plans," *Trusts and Estates,* June 1960, pp. 522-23.

22. SEC Statistical Releases (1960-65).

23. *Commingled Employee Benefit Trust,* Eighth Report, year ending September 30, 1970. (Name withheld by request of bank).

24. The Investment Group of the First National City Bank, *The Anatomy of an Investment,* New York, 1971, p. 27.

25. Voorheis, "Investment Strategy."

26. Federal Deposit Insurance Corporation, *Trust Assets of Insured Commercial Banks,* 1970, Washington, D.C., 1971.

27. During several interviews, the bank vice-presidents in charge of trust departments conservatively estimated that commingled funds for employee benefit plans were approximately 9% of total private pension fund assets.

28. "Another Round," *Forbes* (June 1, 1971), p. 58.

29. Hanczaryk, *Bank Trusts,* pp. 8-9.

30. President's Committee, *A Report to the President on Private Plans,* 1965.

31. SEC Release No. 2516.

32. U.S. Senate, *Economics of Aging,* p. 1582.

33. U.S., Congress, Joint Economic Committee, Subcommittee on Fiscal Policy, *Old Age Income Assurance,* 90th Cong., 1st sess., pt. IV, p. 89.

34. Paul Howell, "Common Stocks and Pension Funds," *Harvard Business Review,* 36, no. 6 (November-December 1958), p. 96.

35. At book value.

36. The latest year in which data are available.

37. SEC Release No. 2516.

38. Besides private noninsured pension funds, this also includes life insurance companies, open-end investment companies, and property and liability insurance companies.

39. At market value.

40. SEC Release No. 2581, April 1971.

41. From the Annual Report of a large West Coast bank.

42. Based on J.J. Jehring, *The Investment and Administration of Profit Sharing Trust Funds,* Evanston, Illinois, 1957, (The Profit Sharing Research Foundation), pp. 130-31.

43. From the 1971 annual report of a medium-sized Pacific Coast bank.

44. Jehring, *Profit Sharing Trust Funds*, pp. 131-32.

45. From the annual report of a medium-sized West Coast bank.

46. Ibid.

47. Stanley Silverberg, "Bank Trust Investments: Their Size and Significance," The *National Banking Review* (June 1964), p. 585, and "Trust Assets Total $288 Billion in Latest Survey," *Trusts and Estates* (January 1972).

48. Irwin Friend, Marshall Blume, and Jean Crockett, *Mutual Funds and Other Institutional Investors: A New Perspective* (New York: McGraw-Hill, 1970), p. x.

49. Frank Voorheis, *Bank Administered Pooled Equity Funds for Employee Benefit Plans* (East Lansing, Michigan: Bureau of Business and Economic Research), 1967.

50. Friend et al., *Mutual Funds*, p. 21.

51. Voorheis, "Investment Strategy," p. 93.

52. SEC *Institutional Investor Study* (1971), p. 408.

53. Voorheis, *Bank Administered Funds*, p. 93.

54. From an interview of a vice-president in charge of trust operations at a large East Coast bank.

55. "Another Round," *Forbes* (June 1, 1971), p. 58.

56. Friend et al., *Mutual Funds*, p. 21. For further discussion on the beta coefficient as a risk measure, see Chapter 3 of this study or: William F. Sharpe, *Portfolio Theory and Capital Markets* (New York: McGraw-Hill, 1970); idem, "Portfolio Analysis," *Journal of Finance and Quantitative Analysis* (June 1967), pp. 76-84; SEC *Institutional Investor Study* (1971), vol. 2, esp. pp. 400-410; Bank Administration Institute, *Measuring the Investment Performance of Pension Funds*, Park Ridge, Illinois, 1968; Jack L. Treynor, "How to Rate Management of Investment Funds," *Harvard Business Review* (January-February 1965), pp. 63-75.

57. A discussion with Harry Markowitz at the Institutional Investor Conference, "The Great Beta Debate," New York City, April 1972.

58. Friend et al., *Mutual Funds*, p. 17.

59. Ibid., p. 2.

60. Ibid., p. 4.

61. Ibid., p. 51.

Chapter 2
Characteristics of the Sample

1. There were three banks which were no longer operating commingled equity funds. Two of these banks merged and the third bank converted its equity fund into a balanced fund. Thus they are no longer eligible for this study.

2. Each bank-administered commingled fund for employee benefit plans must file an annual report with the Comptroller of the Currency. During the correspondence between the writer and the comptroller, it was made clear that the Comptroller's Office would not release these annual reports for inspection. The comptroller felt that this was confidential information. However, his office would release the latest annual report. The rationale behind this decision and the previous one of confidentiality seems conflicting and arbitrary to this writer.

3. Many banks were not eligible to participate since they did not have quarterly data as far back as 1962. Others stated that they did not have "copies to spare." Still other banks have had internal preformance measures of their operation and saw "nothing to gain from participation." There is a possible bias involved if it is assumed that nonparticipation was based upon performance. This explanation for nonparticipation does not seem likely based upon correspondence with these banks.

4. It is interesting to note that throughout the study period the same two commingled equity funds were the two largest funds in total assets.

5. Some of the fiscal years reported did not end at the close of the calendar year; most ended in the latter part of the year. See SEC, *Institutional Investor Study*, vol. 2, p. 459, fn. 145, for further discussion.

Throughout this study the procedure will be followed of merging accounts whose fiscal years end at different times of the calendar year.

Chapter 3
Procedure, Methodology, and Historical Review

1. SEC, *Institutional Investor Study*, vol. 2 (1971), pp. 400-410; Bank Administration Institute, *Measuring the Investment Perform-*

ance of Pension Funds, Park Ridge Illinois, 1968; Michael C. Jensen, "The Performance of Mutual Funds in the Period 1945-1964," *Journal of Finance* 23 (May 1968), pp. 389-416; John C. Bogle, "Mutual Fund Performance Evaluation, Conventional Versus Unconventional," *Financial Analysts Journal*, (November-December 1970), pp. 25-34; Robert Levy, "What Price Performance?" *Barron's* (July 5, 1971), pp. 11-14; William F. Sharpe, "A Simplified Model for Portfolio Analysis," *Management Science*, (January 1963), pp. 277-293.

2. Harry M. Markowitz, "Portfolio Selection," *Journal of Finance*, (March 1952), pp. 77-91; idem, *Portfolio Selection—Efficient Diversification of Investment* (New York: Wiley, 1959).

3. Markowitz, *Portfolio Selection*, p. 100, fn.

4. Sharpe, "Simplified Model"; William F. Sharpe, "Mutual Fund Performance," *Journal of Business* 39 pt. 2 (January 1966), pp. 119-38.

5. Sharpe, "Mutual Fund Performance."

6. John Lintner, "The Valuation of Risk Assets and the Selection of Risky Investments in Stock Portfolios and Capital Budgets," *Review of Economics and Statistics* 67 (February 1965), pp. 13-37.

7. Jack L. Treynor, "How to Rate Management of Investment Funds," *Harvard Business Review* 43 (January-February 1965), pp. 63-75.

8. See: Treynor, "Investment Funds"; Sharpe, "Simplified Model"; SEC *Study*, p. 400. Jensen, "Performance."

9. Treynor, "Investment Funds."

10. Keith V. Smith, *Portfolio Management* (New York: Holt, Rinehart and Winston, 1971). See Chapter 8 for mathematical proof.

11. Jensen, *Performance.*

12. For an excellent discussion of the similarities and differences between Treynor, Sharpe, and Jensen, see: Keith V. Smith, *Portfolio Management* (New York: Holt, Rinehart and Winston, 1971), pp. 187-97.

13. Jack L. Treynor and Kay K. Mazuy, "Can Mutual Funds Outguess the Market?" *Harvard Business Review* 44 (July-August 1966), pp. 131-36; Robert A. Levy, "On the Short-Term Stationarity of Beta Coefficient," *Financial Analysts Journal*, (November-December 1971), pp. 55-62; Marshall E. Blume, "On the Assessment of Risk," *Journal of Finance* (March 1971), pp. 1-10.

14. Smith, *Portfolio Management*, pp. 280-82. This tends to

confirm the fact that most mutual funds are fully diversified with very little residual risk.

15. Others have also contributed significantly to this area, for example see: James Tobin, "Liquidity Preference as Behavior Towards Risk," *Review of Economic Studies* 25 (February 1968), pp. 65-86; Eugene F. Fama, "Risk, Return and Equilibrium: Some Clarifying Comments," *Journal of Finance* 23, no. 1 (March 1968), pp. 29-40.

16. See: Treynor, "Investment Funds"; William F. Sharpe, "Mutual Fund Performance," *Journal of Business* 39, pt. 2 (January 1966), pp. 119-38; Jensen, "Performance"; SEC, *Study*, pp. 400-410; Bogle, "Performance Evaluation."

17. Similar procedures for measuring investment performance are recommended by: Bank Administration Institute, *Measuring Investment Performance*; SEC, *Study*; Wharton School of Finance and Commerce, University of Pennsylvania, *Study of Mutual Funds*, Washington, D.C., G.P.O., 1962. Frank Voorheis, *Bank Administered Pooled Funds for Employee Benefit Plans*, 1967 (East Lansing, Michigan: Bureau of Business and Economic Research).

18. Voorheis, *Pooled Funds.*

19. SEC, *Study.* Also used by: Bank Administration Institute, *Measuring Investment Performance*; Jensen, "Performance"; Friend et al., *Mutual Funds and Other Institutional Investors* (New York: McGraw-Hill, 1970), pp. 54-55.

20. The Standard and Poor's 500 Stock Average is recommended and used in many studies as the market index. See: SEC, *Study*; Jensen, "Performance"; Smith, pp. 243-50.

21. For a further discussion of performance measurements for institutional investors, see: SEC, *Study*; Bogle, "Performance Evaluation"; Friend et al., *Mutual Funds*; Jensen, "Performance."

22. Three-month treasury bill rates will be used, since quarterly data will be used for measuring performance. See SEC, *Institutional Investor Study*, p. 408.

23. Friend et al., *Mutual Funds*, p. 55.

24. Marshall Blume and Irwin Friend, *New Risk-Adjusted Measure of Portfolio Performance*, presented at a seminar at the Wharton School of Finance and Commerce on February 19, 1971, p. 3.

25. Robert Levy, "What Price Performance?" p. 11.

26. See: SEC *Study*, p. 408.

27. Levy, "What Price Performance?" p. 14. (Period studied was thirty-nine months ending March 31, 1971.)

28. SEC, *Study*, p. 459.

29. Stanley Silverberg, "Bank Trust Investments: Their Size and Significance," *The National Banking Review* (June 1964), p. 585. Bank trust departments managed assets of $288 billion in 1970.

30. Edwin W. Hanczaryk, *Bank Trusts: Investment and Performance*, Comptroller of the Currency, 1970.

31. Ibid.

32. Friend et al., *Mutual Funds.*

33. He uses the beta coefficient as a measurement of systematic risk as well as standard portfolios with similar risks for comparison purposes.

34. Friend et al., *Mutual Funds*, table 3-2, appendix, p. 150.

35. Jensen, "Performance."

36. Ibid., p. 415.

37. For example, see: Friend et al., *Mutual Funds.*

38. Voorheis, *Pooled Funds.*

39. SEC, *Study*, vol. 2.

40. Of the forty-eight collective funds, twenty-seven were for employee benefit plans and twenty-one were common trust funds.

41. The SEC study is using the beta coefficient as a measurement of systematic risk and alpha (α) as a measurement of performance.

42. SEC, *Study*, table 5-23, p. 466.

43. Ibid.

44. Ibid., p. 462, see table 5-23, p. 467.

45. Voorheis, *Pooled Funds*, p. 93.

Chapter 4
Investment Performance

1. Paul L. Howell, "Common Stocks and Pension Fund Investment Policies," *Harvard Business Review* 36 (November-December, 1958), p. 93.

2. Irwin Friend, Marshall Blume, and Jean Crockett, *Mutual Funds and Other Institutional Investors: A New Perspective* (New York: McGraw-Hill, 1970), p. 55.

3. Technique recommended by Bank Administration Institute in *Measuring Investment Performance of Pension Funds* (1968).

Used by: SEC *Institutional Investor Study* (1971). See especially Vol. 2, pp. 400-410; M. Jensen, "Performance of Mutual Funds in the Period 1945-1964," *Journal of Finance* (May 1968), pp.

389-419; Robert Levy, "What Price Performance?" *Barron's*, July 5, 1971, pp. 11-14.

4. See Chapter 3 for a full discussion of methodology.

5. The combinations equivalent to a high-risk portfolio may imply a negative holding of the risk-free asset, that is, there is borrowing to leverage the market portfolio. The equivalent risk mixture is found from the extent to which movements in the market as a whole are related to the particular portfolio. For example, if the return on the portfolio is completely independent of the return on the market as a whole, the return on the S & P index gets a zero weight in constructing an "equivalent risk" return. Similarly, if an increase in return of 1% (net of the risk-free rate) in the S & P always is associated with an increase in the portfolio rate of return of 1% (again net of the risk-free rate), the portfolio would be compared with the S & P itself. In this case, the portfolio could outperform the S & P index by having a rate of return that was always at a higher level. For example, it could have successive returns of 5, 8, and 3%, while the S & P had returns of 4, 7, and 2%.

See SEC, *Study*, p. 461.

6. Jensen, "Mutual Funds," p. 406.

7. Levy, "Performance," p. 14. Used over 300 funds 1969-71 (3-year) period.

8. SEC, *Institutional Study* (1967-69), p. 466.

9. Used same methodology for each subperiod as for the entire examination period January 1, 1962, through September 30, 1970.

10. SEC *Institutional Study*; Jensen, "Mutual Funds"; Levy, "Performance."

11. The methodology used to measure performance is described in Chapter 3.

12. For example, see: Wharton, *Study*, 1962; Friend et al., *Mutual Funds*; SEC, *Study*.

13. Voorheis, *Pooled Funds*, 1967.

C. Hoff Stauffer, Jr. and Robert C. Vogel, *Parameters of Mutual Fund Performance*, Wesleyan University, Middletown, Conn., 1969 (Mimeographed). The Voorheis study covers the 1960-64 period, while the Stauffer and Vogel paper covers the 1955-64 period.

14. SEC, *Study*.

15. Stauffer and Vogel, *Parameters of Mutual Fund Performance*.

16. Performance = $a + b_1$ (beta) + b_2 (Activity) + b_3 (bank size)

$$+ b_4 \text{ (fund size)} + b_5 \text{ (diversification)}$$
$$+ b_6 \text{ (growth rate)}.$$

17. Study Periods:

1. January 1, 1962-September 30, 1970
2. January 1, 1962-December 31, 1965
3. January 1, 1966-September 30, 1970

18. SEC, *Study*, p. 461.

19. SEC, *Study*, p. 326.

20. Marshall Blume and Irwin Friend, "New Look at Capital Asset Pricing Model," working paper, Rodney L. White Center for Financial Research of the Wharton School (1972).

21. Ronald Ofer, "Risk, Return and Gross Expectation in the Stock Market," unpublished paper, Wharton School of Finance, University of Pennsylvania (1972).

22. Blume and Friend, *Pricing Model*.

23. SEC, *Study*, p. 462.

24. SEC, *Study*, pp. 331 and 467. Friend, *Mutual Funds*, p. 60. Wharton, *Study* (1962).

25. For the 1966-70 period, the relationship between performance and fund size is statistically significant at the 90% level. That is, there is a weak inverse relationship between performance and fund size for this period. One possible explanation is that the smaller-sized funds had greater flexibility and exercised it prudently during this period.

26. Friend et al., *Mutual Funds*, p. 60.

27. SEC, *Study*, p. 467.

The SEC also found that there was no relationship between performance of investment advisory firms and the size of the investment complex administering these funds; p. 331.

28. Not significant at the 1% level.

29. Blume and Friend, *Pricing Model*; Ofer, *Risk, Return*.

30. SEC, *Study*, p. 462.

31. SEC, *Stock Transactions of Financial Institutions 1971* (April 1972), Table 3.

The portfolio activity rate differs slightly from the turnover rate in that the former includes the results from net accumulations or liquidations while the latter rate does not. The correlation between these two measures is 0.98.

32. Ibid.

33. Stauffer and Vogel, *Parameters of Mutual Fund Performance*.

34. Friend et al., "Mutual Funds," p. 62; Wharton, *Study* (1962).

35. Wharton, *Study* (1962).

36. O.A. Vasicek and J.A. McQuown, "The Efficient Market Model," *Financial Analysts Journal* 28, no. 5. (1972), p. 76.

37. Friend et al., *Mutual Funds*, p. 60; SEC, *Study*, p. 332.

38. SEC, *Study*, p. 332.

39. Adolf A. Berle, "Corporate Power," *The Center Magazine*, January 1969, p. 77.

40. *t* value = 1.143 which is not statistically significant.

Chapter 5
Summary and Conclusions

1. Securities and Exchange Commission, *Private Noninsured Pension Funds 1971*, Release No. 2581, April 1972.

2. During interviews with this writer, several bank vice-presidents in charge of trust operations estimated that 9% of all pension assets were in the form of commingled funds.

3. Study period was January 1, 1962 to September 30, 1970.

4. Bank size is defined as total deposits for the year ending December 31, 1970.

5. Also used by: Jensen, "Mutual Funds"; Bank Administration Institute, *Measuring the Investment Performance of Pension Funds*; Levy, "Performance."

6. Jensen, "Mutual Funds," p. 394.

7. Ibid., p. 393.

8. For example see: Friend et al., *Mutual Funds*; Jensen, "Mutual Funds"; SEC, *Study*; Levy, "Performance."

9. SEC, *Study*, p. 461.

Bibliography

Bibliography

Books

Andrews, Victor; Friend, Irwin; and Minsky, Hyman. *Private Capital Markets.* Englewood Cliffs, N.J.: Prentice-Hall, 1964.

Berle, Adolf A. *Power without Property.* New York: Harcourt, Brace and World, 1959.

Bernstein, Merton. *The Future of Private Pensions.* Glencoe, Ill.: Free Press of Glencoe, 1964.

Brealey, Robert A. *An Introduction to Risk and Return from Common Stocks.* Cambridge, Mass.: M.I.T. Press, 1969.

Cagan, Phillip. *The Effect of Pension Plans on Aggregate Savings: Evidence from a Sample Survey.* New York: National Bureau of Economic Research, 1965.

Friend, Irwin; Blume, Marshall; and Crockett, Jean. *Mutual Funds and Other Institutional Investors, A New Perspective.* New York: McGraw-Hill, 1970.

Goldsmith, Raymond W. *Financial Intermediaries in the American Economy since 1900.* Princeton, N.J.: Princeton University Press, 1958.

Harbrecht, Paul. *Pension Funds and Economic Power.* New York: Twentieth Century Fund, 1959.

Holland, Daniel M. *Private Pension Funds: Projected Growth.* New York: National Bureau of Economic Research, 1966.

Jehring, J.J. *The Investment and Administration of Profit Sharing Trust Funds.* Evanston, Ill.: The Profit Sharing Research Foundation, 1957.

Markowitz, Harry M. *Portfolio Selection.* New York: John Wiley and Sons, 1959.

Measuring the Investment Performance of Pension Funds. Park Ridge, Ill.: Bank Administration Institute, 1968.

Metzger, Bert L. *Investment Practices, Performance and Management of Profit Sharing Trust Funds.* Evanston, Ill.: Profit Sharing Research Foundation, 1969.

Murray, Roger F. *Economic Aspects of Pensions: Summary Report.* New York: National Bureau of Economic Research, Columbia University Press, 1968.

Sharpe, William F. *Portfolio Theory and Capital Markets.* New York: McGraw-Hill, 1970.

85

Smith, Keith V. *Portfolio Management*. New York: Holt, Rinehart and Winston, 1971.

Voorheis, Frank L. *Bank Administered Pooled Equity Funds for Employee Benefit Plans*. East Lansing, Michigan: Michigan State Business School Press, 1967.

Wood, R. Norman. *Measuring the Investment Yield of Pension Funds*. New York: Alexander and Alexander, 1968.

Journals and Periodicals

"Annual Survey of Bank Administered Pooled Funds for Employee Benefit Plans." *Trusts and Estates* (June 1960).

"Another Round." *Forbes*, June 1, 1971.

Berle, A.A. "Corporate Power." *The Center Magazine*, January 1969.

Blume, Marshall E. "On the Assessment of Risk." *Journal of Finance* (March 1971)

Bogle, John C. "Mutual Fund Performance Evaluation, Conventional Versus Unconventional." *Financial Analysts Journal* (November-December 1970), 25-34.

Cummings, F. "Pensions Vesting, Funding and Portability." *Columbia Journal of World Business* (September-October 1968).

Fama, Eugene F. "Risk, Return and Equilibrium: Some Clarifying Comments." *Journal of Finance* 23 (March 1968), 29-40.

Gibb, W.T. "Critical Evaluation of Pension Plans." *The Journal of Finance* 23, no. 2 (May 1968).

Hartwell, J.M. "Performance: Its Promise and Problems." *Financial Analysts Journal* (March-April 1969).

Homer, S. "Impact of Corporate Pension Funds on the Equity and Bond Markets." *The Commercial and Financial Chronicle* (February 28, 1967).

Howell, P. "Common Stocks and Pension Fund Investing." *Harvard Business Review* 36, no. 6.

Jensen, Michael. "Performance of Mutual Funds in the Period 1945-1964." *Journal of Finance* (May 1968), 389-419.

Levy, R.A. "Is Performance Fund Trading Gainful or Wasteful?" *The Institutional Investor* (December 1967).

_____. "On the Short-Term Stationarity of Beta Coefficient." *Financial Analysts Journal* (November-December 1971), 55-62.

_____. "What Price Performance?" *Barron's*, July 5, 1971, pp. 11-14.

Lintner, John. "The Valuation of Risk Assets and the Selection of Risky Investments in Stock Portfolios and Capital Budgets." *Review of Economics and Statistics* 67 (February 1965), 13-37.

Markowitz, Harry M. "Portfolio Selection." *Journal of Finance* (March 1952), 77-91.

McCandlish, R.W. "Some Methods for Measuring Performance of a Pension Fund." *Financial Analysts Journal* (November-December, 1965).

Murray, R.F. "Pension Funds in the American Economy." *The Journal of Finance* 23, no. 2 (May 1968).

"Pension Funds." *Economic Review* (November 1968).

Sharpe, William F. "Mutual Fund Performance." *Journal of Business* 39, pt 2 (January 1966), 119-38.

_____. "Portfolio Analysis." *Journal of Finance and Quantitative Analysis* (June 1967), 76-84.

_____. "A Simplified Model for Portfolio Analysis." *Management Science* (January 1963), 277-93.

Silverberg, Stanley. "Bank Trust Investments: their Size and Significance." *The National Banking Review* (June 1964).

Tobin, James. "Liquidity Preference as Behavior Towards Risk." *Review of Economic Studies* 25 (February 1968), 65-86.

Treynor, Jack L. "How to Rate Management of Investment Funds." *Harvard Business Review* (January-February 1965), 63-75.

_____, and Mazuy, Kay K. "Can Mutual Funds Outguess the Market?" *Harvard Business Review* 44 (July-August 1966), 131-36.

"Trust Assets Total $288 Billion in Latest FDIC Survey." *Trusts and Estates* (January 1972).

Vasicek, O.A., and McQuown, J.A. "The Efficient Market Model." *Financial Analysts Journal* 28, no. 5 (September-October 1972), 71-84.

Voorheis, Frank L. "Investment Strategy of Pooled Funds." *MSU Business Topics* (Spring 1969).

Public Documents

The Internal Revenue Code: 1954. Washington, D.C.: G.P.O., 1954.

The 100 Largest Retirement Plans 1960-1968. Washington, D.C.: G.P.O., 1969.

President's Committee on Corporate Pension Funds and Other

Private Retirement and Welfare Programs. *Public Policy and Private Pension Programs, A Report to the President on Private Employee Plans*. Washington, D.C.: G.P.O., 1965.

Securities and Exchange Commission, *Institutional Investor Study Report*. Washington, D.C.: G.P.O., 1971.

Securities and Exchange Commission. *Private Noninsured Pension Funds*, Statistical Series Releases Nos. 1533, 2132, 1533, 2437 and 2581. Washington, D.C.: G.P.O., 1958, 1966, 1967, 1970, and 1971.

Trust Assets of Insured Commercial Banks, 1970. Washington, D.C.: G.P.O., 1971.

U.S. Congress. Joint Economic Committee. *Investment Policies of Pension Funds*. Washington, D.C.: G.P.O., 1970.

U.S. Congress, Joint Economic Committee. *Old Age Income Assurance, pt. IV*. Washington, D.C.: G.P.O., 1967.

U.S. Congress. Joint Economic Committee. *Private Pension Plans, Part 2*. Washington, D.C.: G.P.O., 1966.

U.S. Congress. Senate. Committee on Banking and Currency. *Institutional Investors and the Stock Market: 1953-1955*. Washington, D.C.: G.P.O., 1956.

U.S. Congress. Senate. Special Committee on Aging. *Economics of Aging; Toward a Full Share in Abundance, pts. 10A and 10B Pension Aspects*. 91st Cong., 2nd sess. Washington, D.C.: G.P.O., 1970.

U.S. Treasury Department. *101st Annual Report*. Comptroller of the Currency. Washington, D.C.: G.P.O., 1963.

Miscellaneous

Collective Investment Funds: Operated under or in General Conformity with Regulation 9 of the Comptroller of the Currency, 1971. American Bankers' Association.

Discussion with Harry Markowitz at the Institutional Investor Conference, "The Great Beta Debate," New York City, April 1972.

Inland Steel Company v. National Labor Relations Board. 170 F.2d. 247 (7th Cir. 1948) Cert. Denied 336 U.S. 960 (1949).

Interviews with eight New York City bank vice-presidents in charge of trust operations. August 1-15, 1971.

"Methods of Measuring Portfolio Performance." Seminar sponsored by Merrill Lynch, Pierce, Fenner and Smith, Inc., October 1967.

Moody's Bank Stock Annual, 1972. Moody's and Company, New York, 1972.

New York Times. "Investment Yields of Pension Funds Growing concern of Wage Earners." November 16, 1970.

New York Times. "Pension Funds Lead Rise on Institutional Trading." March 1, 1971.

New York Times. "Wharton Seminar Challenges Popular Investment Gauges." February 22, 1971.

Public Law 72 Stat. 997 as amended by the Welfare Pension Plans Disclosure Act Amendment of 1962 (P.L. 87-420, 76 Stat. 35).

Reports and Unpublished Papers

The Anatomy of an Investment. The Investment Group of First National City Bank, New York, 1971.

Blume, Marshall, and Friend, Irwin. "New Look at the Capital Asset Pricing Model." Working paper. Rodney L. White Center for Financial Research of the Wharton School of Finance and Commerce, University of Pennsylvania, 1972.

_____. "New Risk-Adjusted Measure of Portfolio Performance." Unpublished paper presented at the Wharton School of Finance and Commerce Seminar on February 19, 1970.

Donaldson, Lufkin and Jenrette, Inc. *Seventh Annual Pension Conference Summary of Proceedings.* New York, 1970.

Hoff Stauffer, C., Jr. and Vogel, Robert C. *Parameters of Mutual Fund Performance.* Middletown, Conn.: 1969. (Mimeographed.)

Institutional Holdings of New York Stock Exchange Listed Stocks 1970. The New York Stock Exchange. New York, February 1971.

Institutions and the Stock Market. The New York Stock Exchange. New York, March 1968 and February 1969.

Malca, Edward. "Noninsured Private Pension Funds as an Institutional Investor." (Unpublished paper, New York, 1969).

Natrella, V. *Implications of Pension Fund Accumulations.* Proceedings of the American Statistical Association, 1957.

Ofer, Ronald. "Risk, Return and Gross Expectation in the Stock Market." (Unpublished paper presented at the Wharton School of Finance, University of Pennsylvania, 1972.)

Index

91

About the Author

Edward Malca is assistant professor of economics at Richmond College of the City University of New York. Professor Malca received the Ph.D. in 1973 from The City University of New York. Besides his teaching position, Dr. Malca is also President of Malca Investment Advisory Service, a firm which specializes in money management. Furthermore, he has had experience in the research department of a highly respected Wall Street investment banking firm. Dr. Malca has contributed to the Wall Street Journal and The Commercial and Financial Chronicle, as well as to other professional journals. He is a member of both The American Finance Association and The American Economic Association.